You Don't Know What War Is

YEVA SKALIETSKA

BLOOMSBURY
CHILDREN'S BOOKS
LONDON OXFORD NEW YORK NEW DELHI SYDNEY

BLOOMSBURY CHILDREN'S BOOKS
Bloomsbury Publishing Plc
50 Bedford Square, London, WC1B 3DP, UK
29 Earlsfort Terrace, Dublin 2, Ireland

BLOOMSBURY, BLOOMSBURY CHILDREN'S BOOKS
and the Diana logo are trademarks of Bloomsbury Publishing Plc

First published in Great Britain 2022 by Bloomsbury Publishing Plc

Translation by Cindy Joseph-Pearson

This book is based on real events as the author remembers them.
However, the names and identifying characteristics of certain individuals,
including all minors and people still based in Ukraine, have been changed
to protect their privacy.

A catalogue record for this book is available from the British Library

ISBN: 978-1-5266-5993-4
eBook: 978-1-5266-6014-5

2 4 6 8 10 9 7 5 3 1

Art direction and typesetting by Katie Knutton

Printed and bound by CPI Group (UK), Croydon CRO 4YY

To find out more about our authors and books visit
www.bloomsbury.com and sign up for our newsletters

For Granny

You Don't Know What War Is

Foreword

You don't know what war is.

It's a good title, a statement, a challenge – words spoken from the heart of someone who does know. We read this book and hear Yeva's voice, loud and clear, telling us the truth. After we have read it, we may still not know what war is, but we understand so much more how it is for those, young and old, families and communities, who have lived through war and are still living through it today. Once read, we will have lived it with Yeva, through her words. Once read, we don't forget. Yeva's utterly compelling story stays with us: one young writer's descent from everyday life into hell, and ultimately, into salvation.

I have written often about war in my stories: ancient wars; world wars; of man's inhumanity to man; of our courage to fight on when all seems lost; of our ability to endure suffering and grief; of our will to survive, to make peace and seek reconciliation. But I have never known war, not at first hand as Yeva has.

I was born in 1943. I was evacuated, was in a sense a refugee, but I have no memory of it. I grew up in post-war London, and that I do remember. There was the ruin of war all about me, a bombsite next to our house where we played – played war-games mostly. There was grief in my mother's face when she spoke of her brother Pieter, who was a wonderful young actor, killed in the RAF aged twenty-one. His photo was always gazing out at me from our mantlepiece. I never knew him. But I know and remember his face now better than any other relative. He stayed the same, never grew old.

Then there was the wounded soldier I'd see on the way to school, sitting on the pavement outside the shop, medals pinned on his jacket, his dog curled up beside him. I'd cross the street often, partly to avoid the dog, but mostly so that I didn't have to look again at his neatly folded empty trouser leg and be reminded again of what war did to human flesh.

My whole family was fractured by war. My father survived it, but his marriage to my mother didn't. War lingers on, goes on wrecking lives, I discovered, long after the fighting has stopped. So it is hardly surprising that I have often written about war, and about our longing for an end to it, for reconciliation and peace.

It is not surprising either that this unique book of Yeva's has made such a huge impression on me. No fiction I could write about war can carry the same intensity or power as her first-hand account of the shattering effect of war on her life, on her family, her friends, her community, her country. Here is an insight into war as it happens to her, as the world falls about around her.

For us all, Yeva's diary is a reminder that war is not a story told by journalists, nor by TV or films or history or fiction. It is lived day-by-day, night-by-night. In Yeva's book it is lived viscerally, in front of our eyes, becomes immediate, will not allow us to look away. Lives and worlds are destroyed. Yeva, like Anne Frank, speaks a truth that all of us, young and old, must listen to. Her words will bring understanding, and in time, reconciliation, because anyone who reads them will know and remember what war really is for those who live it, and will remind us too that hope does spring eternal.

Michael Morpurgo
July, 2022

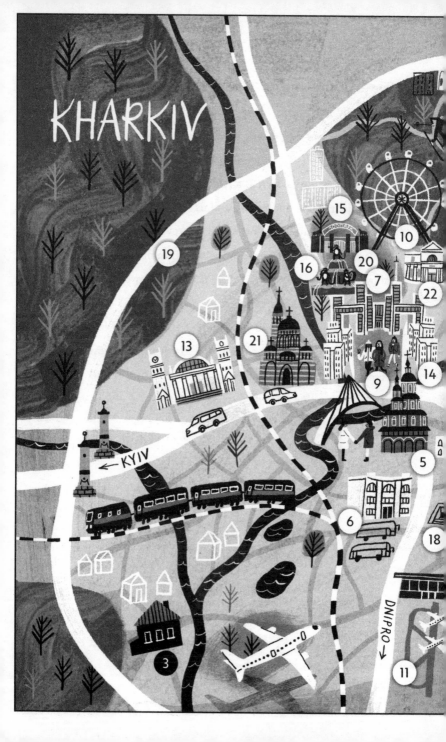

Key

1. **Yeva's flat**
2. **Yeva's school**
3. **Inna's house**
4. Nikolsky Mall
5. Assumption Cathedral
6. Central Bus Station
7. Derzhprom
8. Feldman Ecopark
9. Freedom Square
10. Gorky Park
11. Kharkiv Airport
12. Kharkiv City Children's Hospital
13. Kharkiv Train Station
14. Kharkiv University
15. Kharkiv Zoo
16. Monkey Fountain
17. Opera and Ballet Theatre
18. Prospekt Haharina Metro Station
19. Kharkiv Ring Road
20. Shevchenko City Gardens
21. Svyato-Pokrovsky Monastery
22. The Wedding Palace

Prologue

Prologue

Everyone knows the word 'war'. But very few people understand what it truly means. You might say that it's horrible and frightening, but you don't know the true scale of fear it brings. And so, when you find you suddenly have to face it, you feel totally lost, walled in by fright and despair. All of your plans are interrupted without warning by destruction. Until you've been there, you don't know what war is.

Prologue

BEFORE

14 February 2022

LEADERS IN FINAL PUSH TO AVERT
UKRAINE INVASION

– The Times

BIDEN'S NATIONAL SECURITY ADVISER
SAYS RUSSIA COULD INVADE UKRAINE
'ANY DAY NOW'

– CNN

PRESIDENT DECLARES FEB. 16 UNITY DAY
FOR UKRAINIANS

– Kyiv Post

COUNTDOWN TO WAR

– Daily Mirror

My Birthday • My Life

I wake up early on the morning of 14 February. Today is my birthday. I'm twelve – almost a teenager! There's a surprise in my room: balloons! Five of them! There's a silver one, a pink one, a gold one and even a couple that are turquoise. I feel excited, knowing there will be more surprises to come.

Messages are popping up on my phone from people wishing me a happy birthday. Seven people have already texted before I leave the flat. I'm eager to get to school, and when I arrive everyone stops in the corridor to say happy birthday to me. I smile from ear-to-ear all day long until eventually my face actually starts to hurt. I'm celebrating my birthday on Saturday by having a bowling party at Nikolsky Mall. I've given out the invitations and everyone is excited!

After school, I arrive home. I live with my Granny Iryna,

The day has finally arrived! My twelfth birthday! Here I am surrounded by gifts at my bowling party. I'm so lucky.

but when Mum comes to visit from Turkey, I stay with her at my other grandparents', Granny Zyna and Grandad Yosip. Mum's here for my birthday but Dad lives and works abroad and couldn't come this time. Granny Iryna, my aunt and uncle and my little cousin come round for a special birthday tea. I play a waltz by Tchaikovsky and Beethoven's *Für Elise* on the piano. Everyone listens; it feels very peaceful. Then, we have a tea of snacks and sandwiches and, the best part of all, a tasty cake with candles on it!

19 February

The day has finally come and we are going bowling. I love it so much! Launching the heavy balls. Getting high scores. Having fun! We arrive and I meet up with my friends. Many of them give me gifts of money. But one of my classmates really goes above and beyond ... he gives me a beautiful bouquet of flowers and this small, elegant, Italian-made silver chain with a pendant. The joy I feel has no bounds. I thank him a million times and I hope he sees the sincerity in my eyes.

We start the game. I'm first and I'm doing very well because I've been bowling before. I feel quite competitive! I enjoy rolling the ball and I'm impatient for my turn to come round again. Olha is doing great too. Kostya launches the ball at the speed of light but doesn't seem to care about the direction he's throwing it in, so he's not doing very well. Taras has a very curious approach – he thinks he'll get a strike if he takes a running start, and it actually ends up working. I win one of the two rounds, but in the end, despite my competitive feeling, it doesn't really matter who wins, it's just nice to be all together.

20 February

Then comes the next day and Mum goes back to Turkey. My parents separated when I was two and I've been living with Granny Iryna ever since. We're very happy together – just the two of us.

My life is busy. I attend an English class twice a week and I am really enjoying learning the language. Every Sunday, I go down to the city centre for my piano lessons. I pass old houses with large windows and the Wedding Palace, which was built in 1913 – but the thing I like most about the area is all the shops.

Kharkiv[1] has loads of beautiful places: the city centre, the Shevchenko City Garden, the zoo and Gorky Park. The Shevchenko Garden is especially beautiful and has an amazing musical fountain with monkeys playing different instruments. There's also a really cool dolphinarium nearby where you can go and visit dolphins and beluga whales. There is a beautifully paved street that leads up to the Derzhprom, a group of tall buildings in Freedom Square,[2] and whenever Granny and I need to soothe our souls, we visit the Svyato-Pokrovsky Monastery.

Painting is one of my favourite hobbies.

Me in my Kharkiv flat, ready for school.

I am happy at school. I really enjoy learning and having a laugh with my friends, and I always try not to be late for my lessons. I love the breaks between lessons, especially the longer ones, because I always have tons of fun with my best friends, Evhen and Olha – we run wild around the school, spinning about like little rockets.[3] My favourite subjects are geography, maths, English and German. Once the lessons are over, my friends and I walk home together.

I love the living room at mine and Granny Iryna's flat. It's very cosy, with comfy armchairs. I do my homework on a cute little desk, and I've got my easel and oil paints right in the middle of the room. Whenever I feel inspired, I sit down and paint. In the bedroom, I always have my favourite cuddly toy – a pink cat – on the bed. The cat is long (like a sausage), white-bellied and I call her Chupapelya. I don't know why I named her that, or what it even means, but it just stuck.

The windows in the living room look out towards the city and the windows in the bedroom face some houses and huge empty fields that lead on to the border with Russia.

Granny's flat has a big kitchen filled with Italian furniture. There's a tall palm tree in a pot in the corner – we have a lot of plants – and I also really enjoy taking nice warm baths in our huge tub with massage jets. It's such a lovely home and in a great neighbourhood in the north-eastern outskirts of Kharkiv.

I often have lots of homework. Once I'm done with it,

I turn on the TV. And then, I fall into a carefree sleep.

And that's how life is. Sure, there have been some rumours and murmurings about Russia, but they're just that: words. Life on 14 February is normal. And on the 15th, 16th, 17th … and up until the early hours of 24 February 2022, my life is peaceful.

War In Ukraine

24 February 2022

UKRAINE DECLARES STATE OF EMERGENCY BEFORE POSSIBLE RUSSIAN INVASION

– Irish Times

DISTANT BOOMS HEARD IN KHARKIV, UKRAINE'S SECOND-LARGEST CITY

– Washington Post

RUSSIA ON A 'PATH OF EVIL', SAYS UKRAINE PM ZELENSKY

– CNN

RUSSIAN GROUND FORCES CROSS INTO UKRAINE

– Kyiv Post

WORLD FACES 'MOMENT OF PERIL' SAYS UN

– Independent

Day 1

The Beginning • Horror • War •
The Fear in My Eyes

The night had been very ordinary. I was sleeping soundly. But then, for some reason, I woke suddenly very early in the morning. I decided to leave the bedroom and try sleeping in the living room. I laid on the sofa, closed my eyes and started drifting off.

5:10 a.m. I was woken suddenly by a loud metallic sound that echoed through the streets. At first, I thought it was a car being crushed into scrap metal, which would have been weird because I don't live near a scrapyard.

Then I realised it was an explosion.

I saw that Granny was standing by the window, looking toward the Russian border. She was watching missiles flying over the fields. All of a sudden, a massive rocket sped by and exploded with such force that I felt my heart go cold in my chest.

Car alarms were going off. Granny was trying to stay calm. She came over, saying, 'Is Putin really starting a war with Ukraine?'

I was in complete shock. I didn't know what to say. I knew Granny was telling the truth, but it was very hard to believe. I've grown up hearing about war, but I've never been in one. I was terrified.

We didn't have time to think. No one had told us what we should do if a war broke out. None of us were prepared for a war. Not I, not Granny, not our neighbours. We just knew we had to leave the flat and get to our basement.

My hands were shaking, my teeth rattling. I felt squashed by fear. I realised I was having my first ever panic attack. Granny kept trying to calm me down, telling me I needed to focus. Before we left, Granny put a gold crucifix pendant around my neck. I got the necklace when I was christened and I've never worn it. Then Granny hid her jewellery box away in the wardrobe.

I checked my phone. A discussion about what was happening had broken out on our school chat.

Once we were ready, we headed for the basement. When we got inside, I started having the panicky feeling again – I couldn't breathe, my hands turned cold and sweaty.

The war had begun.

Explosions, noises, my heart beating loudly – I couldn't think through the fear and noise. Tears were welling up in my eyes – I was afraid for my loved ones and for myself.

Our basement wasn't built to be a bomb shelter. There were hot and cold pipes all over the place. Tons of dust. A very low ceiling. Tiny windows that looked up to street level. Men stacked sandbags to block them so that no one would get hurt by flying shards of glass if there was a blast. There were quite a few people down there.

After a while, once it all got quiet, I mustered up the courage to leave the basement and go outside. I took my phone out and turned on the news. People were gathering, talking loudly, trying to make sense of what was going on. But then ... shelling, sharp and frequent. We bolted back down to the basement, which is now our bomb shelter.

Then, a third panic attack, tears, more explosions than I could count ...

06:31
Tolya 🌱
I'm afraid of explosions near my house

06:32
Tolya 🌱
A hundred metres away

06:32
☺ **Myron** ☺
I saw tanks

06:32
☺ **Myron** ☺
Another explosion

06:32
☺ **Myron** ☺
And another

06:33
Misha
Yeah

06:33
☺ **Myron** ☺
Crap so what do we do now

06:34
Ruslan
Don't worry guys

06:34
Ruslan
Just keep calm

06:34
☺ **Myron** ☺
Genius. Easy!

06:34
Ruslan
I pray to god that everything will be OK

06:34

Misha
Yeah

06:47

Yeva
Hello everyone, I went outside and it smells of burning

11:30 a.m. Our neighbour went to the shops to withdraw some cash from an ATM, but had no luck – there were Ukrainian fighters with machine guns there, then explosions were going off again and people started running back home. Terrified, our neighbour ran back too. They said there were Ukrainian snipers on the roofs of the apartment blocks.

Hearing this, I rang all of my friends to find out how they were doing. Some of their experiences have been very intense.

My friend from school, Maryna, said it took her ages to get to a bomb shelter because the traffic was so terrible. Olha is holed up at home saying she's not going anywhere. One of my classmates felt his building shake. Another had a bomb explode 100 metres from his house. He felt his windows rattling.

And it is only the beginning of this hell.

12:30 p.m. I persuaded Granny to pop back home for a bit. We had a quick wash and lunch. I grabbed my diary because I want to start writing things down as they are happening. I also took my laptop, paper and pencils in case I want to draw, a bit of food and some pillows and blankets. Then we went back to the basement.

3:20 p.m. We're hearing rumours that thirty minutes from now there will be planes, troops and bombs.

4 p.m. Nothing's happened yet. Everyone's anxiously looking at each other.

Sunny days never used to surprise me. A peaceful sky was nothing out of the ordinary. But it's all changed now. Before, when I'd hear about children being caught up in military combat, I never quite understood how terrible it was. I see it differently now that I've had to spend five hours holed up in a basement. I feel it clearly, with a sense of pain and dread. The world has changed to me; it has all new colours. The blue sky, bright sun, fresh air – it all seems so beautiful. I know now that we should rejoice in it all.

Every hour there's a new rumour on the news. One of them, which I believed at the time, made me think that writing this diary might end up being a waste of time. It was a rumour that Russia had withdrawn its forces from Ukraine and Kharkiv had defended its independence. However, it was quickly proven false because we heard more explosions and shelling.

Right now, I have only one question on my mind: what will the night be like? I've been told that in wartime, nights and mornings are the most frightening because you never know what to expect. I guess we'll have to wait and see.

4:55 p.m. There's fighting. Machine gunfire or missile launches? Unknown.

We find a few sheets of cardboard from old boxes and use them, and the few blankets and pillows we grabbed earlier, to make a sort of bed for us to sleep in. Someone has brought down a table and some chairs, and a few board games to keep us children distracted from what's going on.

The basement has two exits on either side leading out on to the street, but it's too scary to go outside. The basement runs under the entire length of our block of flats, like a long tunnel. The men show us where the toilet is. Everyone understands that we'll be here a while.

The men are putting a lock on one of the doors, so that we can lock up at night. I decide to check if they've also put a lock on the door at the other end of the basement and it turns out not. Then, all of a sudden, my friend Nadya comes bursting through the doors as they are being shut by some of the grown-ups. She hugs me as tight as she can and I hug her back, trying to calm her down; she's shaking. She has heard explosions on the street.

6:40 p.m. It is dark now. I go outside for a breath of fresh air, and it seems quiet. I return to the basement.

Nadya and her family thought they'd pop back home again, but just as they were getting ready to leave … *boom!*

Hiding in the basement under our apartment in the first few hours of the war, playing games with the other children from the neighbourhood to take our minds off what is going on.

… an explosion. They decided to stay put after all.

The adults are all saying the worst is yet to come.

We're told there is now a curfew – from 10 p.m. to 6 a.m.. We're also told that no one is to leave the bomb shelter because they could start shelling at any time. Yeah …

I doubt we'll get much sleep tonight.

9 p.m. I've never felt the time pass by this slowly before. There's constant shelling. Apparently, Russia has Ukraine surrounded. They want Kharkiv's surrender. More shelling. I almost have another panic attack. I sit down next to Granny and she hugs me. We're frightened. There's talk that the water and electricity in the city will have to be cut off tomorrow as they can't keep providing it in a time of war, but we're not giving in to despair. All we can do is pray.

Everyone is minding their own business. Someone's sleeping (or at least pretending to). Others are talking to their friends and family over the phone, trying to figure out what to do next. One person is telling people about the latest news. Some of the older people are cowering in their chairs, not saying a word. Us children are sitting around a table, some are drawing, some are playing cards and I joined a group playing dominoes. Other people are just glued to their phones.

Granny's ringing her friends to see how they're doing. She's asking them if we could meet up and join them at a safer shelter, because we're too close to the action here and the shelling could get worse.

But we're not losing heart because we're a cheerful lot and we support each other.

We're hearing that other countries are now proposing sanctions, while refusing to send more weapons. In some ways, that might be for the best ...

25 February 2022

RUSSIA BATTERS UKRAINE WITH ARTILLERY STRIKES AS WEST CONDEMNS INVASION

– New York Times

ZELENSKY DECLARES GENERAL MOBILISATION IN UKRAINE

– Kyiv Post

BLASTS HEARD IN KYIV AS RUSSIAN FORCES CLOSE IN

– Washington Post

PUTIN INVADES

– Guardian

LANDMARKS TURN YELLOW AND BLUE IN SOLIDARITY WITH UKRAINE

– Independent

Day 2

*A Quiet Night • Fleeing for Safety • Our Lives are
More Important • Moving Places*

The rest of the night was quiet; there was no shelling. Everyone
seemed to be asleep. As for me, I started feeling drowsy around
half ten and managed to nod off. I woke up at 6 a.m..

Granny thinks it will be safe for us to nip home and grab a
bite to eat, wash ourselves and then quickly come back down to
the basement. We can't stay in our flat for too long because it's
not safe up there on the fifth floor.

7:30 a.m. I'm having breakfast – a piece of buttered bread and
some tea. I keep looking out of the window to see if there are
any tanks or missiles. There aren't.

8 a.m. We packed our things. I thought to myself, *have they
stopped bombing?* But then I heard an explosion: *No, they haven't.*

We rushed downstairs and out of the building. It was very cold. To my surprise, it had started snowing – they say it'll keep snowing for the next few days.

I tried to walk like nothing was wrong, though we were afraid they'd start bombing again. But thankfully, it was quiet.

The word 'shelter' has been written across above the little roof-covering above the basement entrance.

I scrolled through the 180 messages sent to the school chat during the night.

One of my friends has been messaging to say he's scared he'll get blown up because he lives so close to the action. Another shared a video of what is happening in Sumy.[4] It looks like the city is on fire. Two of my classmates stayed up messaging each other until midnight.

8:30 a.m. Next time I looked outside, I heard the sound of tanks driving by. They were heading in the direction of Kyiv. I thought I saw something fly through the sky at great speed and I guessed it must be a missile. Who knows if it hit or not. Maybe I'm just being paranoid.

8:40 a.m. I got a call from my classmate Maryna who wanted to tell me her aunt said the shelling will start up again in half an hour. Soon after the call, I fell asleep for about an hour. There wasn't any shelling after all.

Then, we learned that Ukrainian tanks and APCs[5] are

stationed between apartment buildings. We are worried we'll end up being used as human shields. Granny decided she'd ring her friend Inna to see if we could stay with her. We rang the taxi company and waited for what felt like forever for them to get back to us.

When the taxi finally arrived, we got in and set off for Inna's.

I asked Granny, 'What about all our things?'

She replied, 'We'll have to leave them. Our lives are more important!'

I left my friends.

That hurts …

But we do what we have to do to survive. We have to save ourselves at any cost.

As we drove through Kharkiv, I thought it seemed strangely normal, apart from the long queues outside pharmacies and supermarkets. There aren't any fighters by the shops now.

While on the road, we saw an army vehicle that had broken down. Then we saw another one, carrying Ukrainian fighters. 'What on earth are they driving around here for?' I asked. It felt very strange to see them on our normal roads.

'Try not to worry about that,' Granny said.

After about thirty minutes, we arrived at Inna's house in New Bavaria, on the western edge of Kharkiv. It's a cute, cosy little house. It's better here. There has still been some shelling here, but not much. On the other hand, as it's a little higher up the explosions echo around more.

The kitchen is quite spacious, with a large dining table in the middle. The house has three bedrooms, and we picked the one with a large fold-out sofa for us to sleep on. It's a little cold in the room, so we covered the window with a blanket.

The house has a small wood burner near the front door. Out on the terrace, there's a hatch leading to an underground cellar.

In the kitchen, Inna has a beautiful, huge seascape painting with some real seashells attached to it. The painting isn't complete though. Inna knows I can paint, so she suggested I finish it for her. I agreed, because it felt like a good distraction from all the explosions we kept hearing in the distance. I also asked her to give me a little sheet of plywood because I've got an idea: I want to paint an angel on it. I think I'll try and paint it in the style of Gapchinska.[6]

As for the situation back home, which I left barely an hour ago, it's best not to think about it.

My friend Rita and her mum heard from us that things in the city had quieted down a little, so tried to drive to Pisochyn.[7] They set off to get their things but didn't get far. The shelling started up again, heavier than before. Fighters, tanks, bombs, explosions. It was too late for them to go … Everyone was panicking and running towards the nearest basement. We aren't in as much danger here as our friends back in our neighbourhood. What's going to happen? Will they survive? Will our homes? No one can make any promises.

Huge bombs have been found on the streets of Kharkiv.

Me trying to keep calm by painting a mural of the seaside in Inna's kitchen.

As for the rumours about cutting our water and electricity – thankfully those weren't true.

1:30 p.m. It's on the news that fighter planes have taken off from Kursk, Russia, but their destination is anyone's guess. One possibility – they're going to Kyiv, the capital.

I've just realised that my phone charger is still in our basement. My phone doesn't have much battery left. We don't have a lot of food left, either. Thankfully, Inna has a phone charger I can borrow so I don't have to worry about that at least.

Messages keep coming in on the group chat. My friend Polyna texted me to say that there are tanks near our home, driving down Hvardiitsiv-Shyronintsiv Street. I told Granny and Inna this, to which they just said, 'Try not to worry. There's nothing we can do … it is what it is.'

We refuse to panic.

I've heard there are tanks firing just 200 metres away from my school. Myron, my schoolmate, left his basement to get some fresh air. Suddenly, there was a red light, the sound of a missile and machine gunfire. He ran straight back to the basement. Dyana is holed up at her house in Velyka Danylivka, across the road from our neighbourhood in north-east Kharkiv, watching things unfold.

My neighbourhood, North Saltivka,[8] is practically being erased. It is terrible! All the little streets I used to play in, the little courtyards, my favourite pizza place and my school! It was all so beautiful! Such a terrible shame … and for what? The tall block of flats at 60 Natalii Uzhvii Street was hit by a missile. I saw that building – it was fine when we were on our way to Inna's. When I learned that it was destroyed, I got chills. New Bavaria, where we are now, is all quiet, but North Saltivka definitely isn't. The school announced a two-week holiday. Yeaaah … Doesn't sound like much of a holiday …

And now, for some lighter news. We've got the little wood burner going, and it's my job to tend the fire. I keep telling myself it's important to look for the positives, no matter how bad it gets. For now, I'll just enjoy watching the firewood burning in the furnace. We sit round it to keep each other company. It's not so scary when we're together.

I got curious about what the cellar we'll be hiding in is like. I opened the hatch and went down two steps. There was another hatch in front of me, so I unfastened that too. Beyond that was a very deep cellar. I have no doubt that we will be safe here.

7 p.m. It's starting to get dark outside. There has been some shelling. We wonder whether it's our cue to go and hide in the cellar …

7:15 p.m. The explosions are getting louder. We suspect they'll start using Grad systems,[9] and those are not known for their precision.

They're bombing hard around Velyka Danylivka where my

friends Dyana and Tolya live. I hope they're staying strong.

Inna's listening to the explosions and trying to figure out where they land. She's trying to calm Granny down by telling her that they sound far away.

After dinner it feels more relaxed. We talk. I watch Minecraft YouTube videos. Meanwhile the government is telling people to take up arms and join the fight.

7:50 p.m. It's very dark out. The darkest kind of dark. I feel too scared to go outside. Inna's friend has come over so we can all keep each other company.

We're not turning on the news because it just frightens us. I can still feel my heart beating anxiously but I'm trying to calm myself. With the heat from the little wood furnace, I'm feeling sleepier by the second.

9 p.m. Once the fire was out, Inna called me into the living room where it's warmer. I sat on a comfy armchair. I wound down a little and, for a moment, forgot all about the horrors I've been through over the past couple of days.

We said a prayer together and then Inna went to bed.

Everything is silent. We're hoping for a quiet night, just like the one before …

10 p.m. I can barely keep my eyes open any more. I don't think it will be long before I'm fast asleep …

26 February 2022

Day 3

Are We Past the Worst? • *Cry From the Heart* •
Life Goes on • *A Restless Evening*

7:40 a.m. I'm leaning against a wall and I can feel it shaking.
It's terrifying.

'I think they're bombing Zmiiv,'[10] Inna says.

8 a.m. Apparently, the first two days of a war are the hardest, but
we're on day three now.

Inna went out to the shop and came back two hours later.
Food prices have gone up – everything's really expensive now.
Some things aren't even available any more. The shop had a
fresh delivery of bread, but there wasn't enough for everyone.
Everyone is buying vodka.

I'm starting to see that we were right to leave our flat behind
yesterday when we did. I'm so glad we didn't leave it too late like
Rita and her mum who couldn't leave because of the bombing.

Our lives are more important than a few bits of clothing or even the flat itself. It doesn't matter if you haven't got your things or that you've left your home behind. You'll come back one day. It's a difficult thing to get your head around. With each day, I'm learning that life goes on, even in war time. We hang on to the hope that sooner or later, the war will be over.

They bombed the airport. That's quite far away from here, but I could hear the sound of it very clearly. If I can hear it here in New Bavaria then I can't imagine what it would sound like if I was closer to it all. I can't help but wonder how many years it will take to build it all back up again. Who knows?

Last night we thought we heard some army vehicles driving by for the first time here.

I saw this post by Oleksii Potapenko[11] on his Instagram story. I'd call it a cry from the heart:

Why aren't any of the Ukrainian networks showing the sheer hell unfolding in Schastia[12] (Luhansk Oblast)[13] – the people there are living in ruins!

Ukrainian civilians must be evacuated urgently! Why is no one saying anything? Why isn't anyone doing anything? How can you treat your own people this way? As many people as possible must be told about this so that everyone can start doing something! Helping with the evacuation – anything!

We're told that the explosions we heard yesterday were the city ring road getting shelled. Apparently, Ukrainian tanks destroyed the Russian tanks over by Pisochyn and Vysokyi village. Pisochyn has a road that leads to Kyiv and Vysokyi leads to Dnipro.[14] The Russian tanks were headed to Kyiv, but our tanks stopped them ...

1 p.m. There's a big round of explosions. They're not the loudest I've heard but it's frightening nonetheless. They've changed the curfew again – it's now from 6 p.m. to 6 a.m..

They're saying on the news that the Russians have already suffered 3,000 casualties but that the Russian news isn't mentioning that.

I'm thinking about what a beautiful city Kharkiv is ... or was. How much time and money was spent to create a place so perfect, but then, in an instant, it was all blown to hell!

They're shelling civilians more now than they did at the start.

Grandad Yosip told us he's been walking around the streets. We're shocked – there's a war going on and he thought he'd just take a stroll!

I've heard that Tolya's situation back in Velyka Danylivka is getting worse. The bombing there is even heavier. And Myron's dad's friend has a missile lying in the courtyard of his block of flats. I'm scared. We can still hear the explosions, but they're far away.

Rita and her mum decided to take a train to Bezliudivka. As I write this, they're down in the Prospekt Haharina metro station. There are a lot of people there apparently. As they were going down to the station there was a hail of missiles behind them. Thankfully, no one was hurt.

As for our neighbourhood back home, friends say that the buildings are shaking ... My heart is full of fear. What will happen next is anyone's guess ...

3:10 p.m. There's heavy shelling now. We've tidied up the cellar in case we need to stay here a while. The walls are curved, and all around me are crates of glass jars full of all sorts of stuff. Pickled tomatoes and cucumbers, as well as raspberry and apricot jam. Granny and Inna bring in a bench, and I throw some coats over it. It's quite a small room so it's not too cold in here. After sorting the cellar, we climb back up to the house.

3:55 p.m. Two sudden explosions about six kilometres away, so we immediately run to the cellar. It's quiet again now. Down in the cellar, we say a prayer and send it on. Fear engulfs us. We're hoping and praying – that's just about all we can do.

The sun's going down. We want peace. We can't remember our old dreams any more, or all the things we thought to be important. We can't recall our old arguments or troubles. All of those past concerns just don't matter. When there's a war going on, you've only got one goal – staying alive. Everything that seemed hard or bad in the past, becomes trivial. You're afraid for the lives of your loved ones and every day is interrupted by the sound ... *BOOM!* ... You start thinking about how fortunate you are that this one rocket hit far away from you, whilst hiding the terror gripping your heart. You pray all day, asking God for peace. You hold on to every minute, every second of your life …

We keep ringing all of our friends to check up on them, and we learn that the Russians are shelling all over Ukraine. The news is saying there is a full-scale war going on. The words 'full-scale' are frightening. They pour fear into our souls. My soul is screaming. I'm hurting, but I must carry on – stay safe and hope that the war will be over soon, and we will have peace.

I want to take something to calm my nerves but, more than that, I wish this was all just a terrible nightmare I could wake up from.

5:40 p.m. It's dark outside. We got a call from Granny's friend, Nelya. She says there's a Ukrainian tank stationed near the kindergarten and that it keeps shooting at something. Then, we get a call from my teacher at school. She shares a terrifying story with us:

'A nearby garage caught fire. We were holed up in the basement of another garage ourselves, so we realised we weren't safe there any more. We decided to run over to the school basement. As we were running, there were missiles flying just above us. We ran for our lives. Thankfully, we managed to get there without anybody getting hurt.'

I am very scared for her. She's my favourite teacher.

6:57 p.m. Inna made zapekanka[15] for supper and we had it with some raspberry jam and mint tea. I calmed down a little, but then there were more explosions. We're told it is our guys shooting towards Russia from their positions on the city's ring road. There is constant noise from all the planes and missiles. This time last night, it was more quiet, but tonight, it's deafening.

Apparently, a group of saboteurs were caught in Kharkiv. They say they were trying to rig the streets with explosives.[16]

As I write tonight, I don't feel much hope.

Once the shelling had died down, Inna called me into her room. It is a small space with a single window, but it is the safest room in the house. She turned on a little yellow night light. The rest of the lights in the house are turned off to keep the planes from spotting them. I prayed things would stay quiet until morning.

At that very moment, they started bombing the ring road and there were planes flying all around. I tried my best to stay calm but ended up having a little panic attack – I was struggling to breathe and I felt like my chest was being crushed.

They are bombing; we are sitting. I think it will be safer if I lie down. Even though the shelling is far away from here, Granny spots a searchlight from the window and insists on going to the cellar. I go with her.

7 p.m. We're down in the cellar having some tea. Inna refuses to join us because it's quiet now and she's worried that if the

In bed at Inna's house. Feeling hopeless.

house was to collapse from an explosion, we will be trapped and no one will know we are down here.

I called out to Inna to fetch my diary so that I can write things down as they're happening. Things are letting up and I'm starting to relax a bit.

By the way, Rita and her mum made it to the train and now they're safe.

I'm writing in my diary using the little light on my phone.

North Saltivka is being showered with rockets.

We'll leave the cellar to go to bed once it gets quiet.

27 February 2022

**PUTIN DELIBERATELY MAKES DECISIONS
THAT COULD LEAD TO A NEW
WORLD WAR**

- Die Welt

**RUSSIA HITS UKRAINIAN AIRFIELDS AND
FUEL FACILITIES IN WAVE OF ATTACKS**

- Irish Times

TERROR STALKS THE STREETS

- Sunday Times

**'IT'S STOMACH-TURNING':
THE CHILDREN CAUGHT UP IN
UKRAINE WAR**

- Guardian

WELCOME THESE REFUGEES

- Independent

Day 4

An Eventful Night • Hell in North Saltivka •
Scared but Must Venture Out

I slept, waking up at 8 a.m.. This seems late for me now. I rolled over and the sun was shining on me. A bright beam of light fell across my face. To me, it seemed like a sign. I wanted to go outside and enjoy the sunshine. But then I remembered.

It turns out that there was especially heavy bombing last night, far away from here though. I was fast asleep as it was happening. I was just so tired of listening to all the explosions that I must have simply switched off. Velyka Danylivka was on fire. North Saltivka was being shelled by Grads. This was the first time in three days that there was shelling late at night.

I get in touch with my friend Olha. She tells me what has been happening to her. The kindergarten near her had its roof blown off. A nearby building entrance was destroyed in a blast and a man and a woman got hit in the back with debris.

The ambulance took a long time (an hour) to get there and kept refusing to take them but did in the end.

Olha and her family were queueing outside the Equator Mall for ages to do their shopping, but just as she was approaching the till to pay, the electricity cut out. She didn't get her shopping but she'll try again today.

10 a.m. We've run out of water, so we decided to go to the spring. It seemed like the street was totally empty, but we did meet a couple of people. There were explosions, but they were far away. We brought back some water. Inna was showing me around her garden. She has fruit trees growing there, a raspberry bush and a blackcurrant bush – there is also a strawberry patch. She was showing me where she is going to plant some flowers, but then … *BOOM! …BOOM!* … Two explosions very close by! Me and Granny ran to the cellar, though Inna stayed upstairs.

Later, Grandad Yosip sent a picture of a terrible scene. There was a bomb lying on the road right in front of a shop – it was about two metres long. The bomb wasn't armed; it was only a marker.[17]

There are Russian tanks over in the city centre.

We climbed out of the cellar but, fifteen minutes later, I went back down again because there were more sounds.

We are very lucky with our neighbours here; they take care of us, and we take care of them. They bring us food.

10:08
Tolya ☺
Guys, I'm all good for now, half my street was hit, but they didn't touch us

10:08
Tolya ☺
I'm turning off my phone for now, but I might come back later

10:08
Tolya ☺
The lights are out ...

10:08
Tolya ☺
See you later!

10:39
Dyana
Damn

11:08
Polyna ☆
There's shooting here

11:24
Davyd
Hey

11:25
☺ **Myron** ☺
Hello

11:25
☺ **Myron** ☺
Tykhon, is it all quiet there?

11:36
Tykhon
There's fighting over in Alekseevka

11:36
Tykhon
So no, it's not quiet

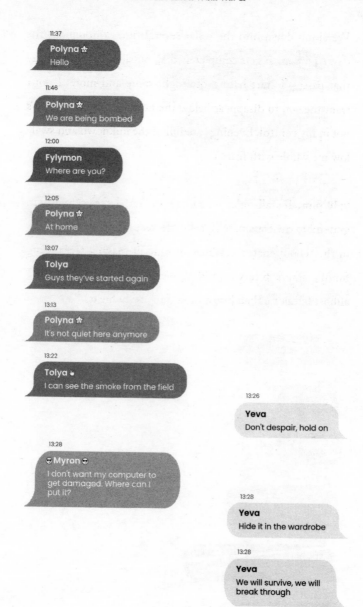

11:37
Polyna ☆
Hello

11:46
Polyna ☆
We are being bombed

12:00
Fylymon
Where are you?

12:05
Polyna ☆
At home

13:07
Tolya
Guys they've started again

13:13
Polyna ☆
It's not quiet here anymore

13:22
Tolya ✌
I can see the smoke from the field

13:26
Yeva
Don't despair, hold on

13:28
☺ Myron ☺
I don't want my computer to get damaged. Where can I put it?

13:28
Yeva
Hide it in the wardrobe

13:28
Yeva
We will survive, we will break through

We climb down into the cellar several times throughout the day. At 6 p.m., it gets completely dark outside. With every day that passes, I start hating the night more and more. I don't want the sun to disappear below the horizon but, sadly, that's not in my control. Evenings are full of the unknown and swallow me whole with fear.

9:30 p.m. It's all quiet where we are and I feel calmer. I'm grateful to my classmate Kyrylo! He keeps posting silly videos in the school chat; recordings of himself making faces using funny camera filters on his phone. I'm laughing so hard I almost fell out of bed just now and my belly hurts.

28 February 2022

PUTIN ISSUES NUCLEAR THREAT

– Daily Telegraph

**MORE THAN 350 CIVILIANS HAVE
BEEN KILLED**

– New York Times

DASH TO THE BORDERS

– Sunday Times

**'WHO ELSE BUT US?': UKRAINE'S
CIVILIANS TAKE UP ARMS**

– Irish Times

**MILITARY AND HUMANITARIAN AID
POURING INTO UKRAINE**

– Kyiv Post

Day 5

*An Unexpected Start • An Attempt to Get
Food and Medicine*

I woke up at 3 a.m.. I was just nodding back off to sleep when fighter jets started dropping bombs. I can feel the anxiety taking over. Every explosion brings a chill through my body. Inna called for us to climb down to the cellar and said she would join us this time. We got down there and stayed put. I can't imagine how dangerous it must be outside if Inna decided to come with us. I drifted off to sleep down there. The curfew's been changed again: 3 p.m. to 6 a.m..

8 a.m. More shelling, but it seems to be far away.

Granny's friend rang us and said a house in Vysokyi village has been destroyed, but there were no casualties apart from a dog. Turns out, that's what all the shelling we just heard was.

Later, Granny and Inna tried going to the shops to get some

food, but it didn't work out.

Granny said, 'I was standing in the queue, and I was very frightened. There was more bombing around us than when we went to get water yesterday. People are still queueing. They've got used to all the shelling. People are prepared to queue in the middle of it all just to get a morsel of food.'

We heard from Granny Zyna. She said that she wanted to break curfew yesterday to go to the pharmacy. She asked Grandad Yosip to go with her, but he said the nearest one was closed. She suggested they go over to another on Heroiv Pratsi. I feel like, if her house were being bombed, she'd be as calm as a boa.[18] Grandad Yosip refused because the curfew is very strict and it isn't safe to go outside. Why the hell are they shelling people who are just trying to buy their medicine?

Today, negotiations are being held between delegations from both the Russian Federation and Ukraine. A block of flats was destroyed this afternoon. There are casualties. Accidents. The bodies aren't taken away. Civilians are being shelled from every direction.

There's a car park next to mine and Granny's building, and the flats behind it were hit in the shelling.

13:43

Polyna ☆
We've dragged our beds into the corridor. It's safer here.

13:43

Nadya
We're getting totally pounded

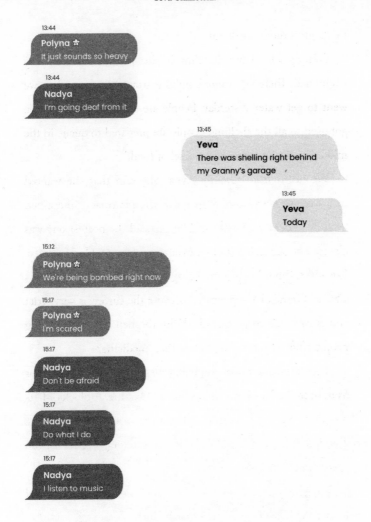

13:44
Polyna ☆
It just sounds so heavy

13:44
Nadya
I'm going deaf from it

13:45
Yeva
There was shelling right behind
my Granny's garage

13:45
Yeva
Today

15:12
Polyna ☆
We're being bombed right now

15:17
Polyna ☆
I'm scared

15:17
Nadya
Don't be afraid

15:17
Nadya
Do what I do

15:17
Nadya
I listen to music

6 p.m. It's dark now. My hatred for the night grows more as every day passes by into darkness.

1 March 2022

RUSSIAN ROCKETS POUND KHARKIV

– Financial Times

ASSAULT INTENSIFIES AS TALKS END

– Wall Street Journal

PUTIN ACCUSED OF WAR CRIMES

– Evening Standard

**'NOBODY IS GOING TO BREAK US':
ZELENSKY ADDRESSES EU PARLIAMENT**

– Irish Times

**UKRAINE RELIEF EFFORTS ACROSS
NORTHERN IRELAND INUNDATED
WITH DONATIONS**

– Independent

Day 6

*A Beautiful Dream • A Terrible Bit of News •
Our Flat is Gone • A Day of Hell From The Sky*

I had a wonderful dream last night. I dreamed of my school –
and, most significantly, of a peaceful sky. Me and my friends
were running around, carefree. It felt like the good old days …

I wish things weren't the way they are now. I'm so tired of
the sound of explosions, I really want to hear the sounds of
peacetime again – birds singing and the sound of rain. It was so
nice before the war … I want to go back to my old life.

The shelling at 6 a.m. this morning was no joke, but it's quiet
now, I think. Even so, Inna and Granny are lining the windows
with tape in case of a blast.

There are planes flying around. In the city centre, Freedom
Square was just destroyed by a single missile strike. There's a
video of the bomb exploding. In it, you can see two cars, one
of which swerves to the side. Some people jump out of it. Two

more people run away from the impact site. They're saying that bombs also hit the zoo, Derzhprom, Gorky Park, the university and the opera house, as well as the Philharmonic.

Everything is happening so quickly.

10 a.m. Inna went to buy some groceries, despite shells hailing down, and, this time, she was successful.

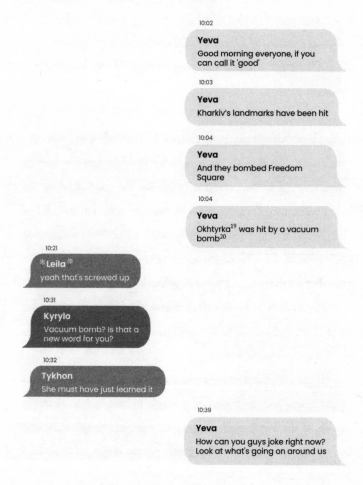

10:02

Yeva
Good morning everyone, if you can call it 'good'

10:03

Yeva
Kharkiv's landmarks have been hit

10:04

Yeva
And they bombed Freedom Square

10:04

Yeva
Okhtyrka[19] was hit by a vacuum bomb[20]

10:21

Leila
yeah that's screwed up

10:31

Kyrylo
Vacuum bomb? Is that a new word for you?

10:32

Tykhon
She must have just learned it

10:39

Yeva
How can you guys joke right now? Look at what's going on around us

10:40

Leila
Yeva, don't mind them they're just idiots

10:40

Yeva
Thank you Leila

10:42

Yeva
By the way, have you seen what's happened to Freedom Square?

10:42

Tykhon
Totalled

10:43

Leila
yeah

11:28

Polyna ☆
Guys. Just now. Rockets flying past.

11:32

Polyna ☆
I'm scared

11:51

Evhen
The kiosk next to my place has been destroyed

11:58

Yeva
Evhen, stay strong, we are with you

12:00

Leila
Everything will be fine

12:36

Evhen
We are on our way to Poltava[21]

13:47

Yeva
My house was hit, my flat doesn't have a balcony any more 😭😭😭

12 p.m. We've had some traumatising news. We got a call from one of our neighbours, telling us that my kitchen has been hit by a missile. We're told there are emergency services outside our block of flats.

As for the kind of missile that caused all this, the emergency workers are saying that it was a submunition[22] from a cluster bomb[23] (which are banned under the Geneva Convention).[24] They urgently need to get inside to check that there aren't any unexploded submunitions threatening to level the entire building.

Granny spent ages on the phone trying to get someone to collect the keys from here, but no one can help so they had to break into the flat. There weren't any unexploded submunitions, but the kitchen's been blown to pieces and the hallway is full of debris.

This really hurts. I spent my childhood there. Attacking my home is the same as attacking a piece of me. I feel like my heart is being squashed.

There were such memories there! Our Italian furniture, our fancy dinner sets, the glass table. All those memories blown to bits. Tears are streaming down my face, and that's only a fraction of my sorrow. I don't care as much about the things themselves as much as I care about the memories they held. I grew up there, and it has simply been destroyed!

There isn't much left of the flat. Why doesn't anyone care? Why? Do you enjoy fighting in cities, destroying everything in

Our flat has been hit by a missile. I'm in shock.

your wake, instead of fighting in the battlefields? Kharkiv is being destroyed bit by bit.

If you want a detailed description of what happened to my flat, then read on – we've been given all the details... The balcony, kitchen and the part of the hallway leading into it were all destroyed. Bits of plaster, rubble and broken glass fill the hallway. My bedroom windows were blown off, but the room itself seems intact. The living room, along with its windows, was spared. The front door was so bashed up that even if Granny had managed to get the key over there, it wouldn't have helped. The emergency workers closed the front door as best they could and fixed it in place with tape. We want to weld the door shut. Will there be anything left in our flat after the war?

7 p.m. Today has been a day of constant activity in the air. As usual, once it got dark outside, Inna's friend went back home. Granny was in the kitchen making tea when suddenly she saw a giant drone. All of its lights were flashing, and it flew so low over the house that she dropped to the floor. Inna and I were in her little room when we heard it. It sounded strange, not like a plane at first. We got down on the floor. We didn't rush down to the cellar this time, because if the house got blown up, no one would know that we were down there. We would just get buried. The drone did a circle around the area, dropping bombs as it went. Rivers of tears. I lay on the bed and, for the first time in my life, I just thought about how I really want to live. My heart stops every time another bomb gets dropped. I was holding on to every minute, every second. I've never been this close to death before. I was praying for the drone to fly away and for the bombs not to hit the house, just praying, *God, help me*. I couldn't breathe.

After a while everything went quiet.

Eventually I managed to calm down.

I checked my phone and Evhen was still on his way to Poltava. He sent a photo he'd taken of a flying missile.

And Dyana said as she was leaving Velyka Danylivka there were houses burning behind her.

We went down to the cellar after all. I tried to get some rest down there, but I couldn't sleep so we ended up going back upstairs.

2 March 2022

**DESPERATE RUSH FOR THE LAST
TRAIN FROM KYIV**

– Guardian

**ZELENSKY PLEADS WITH WEST TO
PREVENT GENOCIDE**

– Daily Telegraph

**KYIV AND KHARKIV NOW UNDER SIEGE IN
RUSSIAN INVASION**

– Irish Times

RUSSIA HAMMERS CIVILIAN TARGETS

– Wall Street Journal

**HEAVY RUSSIAN LOSSES CLAIMED
BY UKRAINE**

– Kyiv Post

Day 7

Another Dream, But Not as Sweet • Are we Doomed? •
A Lucky Turn • We're Leaving Kharkiv

I had a dream. We were in our Toyota, driving down to our bombed-out flat.[25] We went inside, and the hallway was filled with rubbish. We went into the kitchen, and found that the cupboards were undamaged. The table was broken. I started filming. Suddenly, there was a missile flying towards the neighbouring building. I couldn't talk. That's where the dream ended.

There was artillery fire this morning.

The internet was cut off at 6 a.m..

Because of the air raids, people are starting to panic buy, emptying the shops of food.

10 a.m. Granny and I want to leave Kharkiv for Western Ukraine, so we are further from the Russian border. We are calling everyone we know to figure out how we can do this.

People say we should stay put for now. Many of my schoolmates are going to Dnipro or Poltava first, and on to Western Ukraine from there.

Inna has seen many cars leaving the city. Some have the word 'children' written on them on every side.

They're saying that the trains evacuating people have had the seats taken out. Thirty to forty hours standing up. We decided we'd stay in Kharkiv for now.

1 p.m. After thinking about it some more, we decided that we should go to Lviv.[26] There's a scary rumour they could start purging Kharkiv in a few days in order to get everyone to surrender quickly. I spent half the day trying to call a taxi company, but every time they'd pick up, we'd get cut off. Mum kept sending us phone numbers for drivers in Kharkiv, but none of them were picking up. Eventually, I got through to someone who agreed to take us to the train station, but he could only do it in a couple of days. Another number picked up, but we got cut off again. I've sent more messages to Mum and Dad, asking for help, but they're not going through.

3 p.m. I've fallen into a depression. All I can think is *I'm scared, we are doomed* in a loop. I've stopped talking. My face feels like it will never smile again. Thinking about painting my Gapchinska angel makes me feel a bit better. I must not lose hope. I'll keep praying that we'll make it to Lviv, or even out of the country.

We'll continue doing everything we possibly can although we're under curfew right now, so can't go to the southern train station to leave Kharkiv just yet.

8 p.m. We kept hoping and praying that we could find a way to leave this city. And then, at around 4 p.m. we had a lucky turn. Inna's daughter, Lukyia, sent us phone numbers for two Red Cross volunteers.[27] We only managed to reach one of them, but he agreed they would pick us up in fifteen minutes and take us to Dnipro. Oh joy! We gathered our things and went to stand on the street to wait for the car. I had to leave my painting of the angel behind. Pity. I didn't get to finish a part of her dress. Inna came to see us off, but she said she wouldn't be coming with us. Then, suddenly, she ran back into the house, telling us not to wait for her if the volunteers come before she got back. Granny and I heard the sound of explosions. We didn't know if the car would be able to find its way to us or not. We were very nervous and kept asking God for help. We got a call from the volunteers, Todor and Oleh. I didn't know how to give them directions, but then I saw a Volkswagen with a red cross on it and I knew it was them. We got in the car at 4:50 p.m.. Granny asked them to go round the corner so that we could say goodbye to Inna, but then, there she was, running towards us. She had decided to go with us to Dnipro after all! She has family there and so we decided to get dropped off at their place. Inna didn't take anything with her, just her passport, which is what she'd run back for.

The kind Red Cross volunteers who rescued us.

We set off. We passed twelve checkpoints[28] on our way. As we got closer to Dnipro, there was a huge line of cars, several kilometres long, trying to get into the city. We drove around them. It got dark and started raining. We entered the city. It was quiet there; heaven for my ears. The buildings were whole and undamaged. A peaceful sky – what else can you ask for?

We thanked Todor and Oleh for bringing us to this safe place. They said there was no need to pay them, and we said our goodbyes.

We met up with Inna's family. I felt happy. There is a beautiful park just over the road behind us. We went into the flat and told everyone about what we've been through. It took me a while to relax.

We still want to get to Western Ukraine, but we'll think about that tomorrow. For now, we just want to enjoy a peaceful night here with Inna's family.

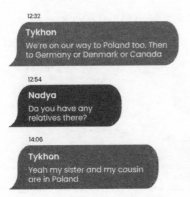

12:32

Tykhon
We're on our way to Poland too. Then to Germany or Denmark or Canada

12:54

Nadya
Do you have any relatives there?

14:06

Tykhon
Yeah my sister and my cousin are in Poland

19:46

Nadya
Did you take your cat?

20:01

Tykhon
No

20:35

Yeva
Hello everyone. I'm in Dnipro

21:43

Dyana
Hi, me, my parents and my dog are leaving Velyka Danylivka where it was bombed two days ago

21:43

Dyana
Yeva – Forever? Or just for the war?

21:43

Dyana
Are you in Kharkiv, Ella?

21:43

✷ Ella ✷
No

21:43

Dyana
Where then?

21:45

✷ Ella ✷
In Lviv

21:45

Dyana
Ah OK. I heard there's no shooting there, only constant sirens and that's it. Or is there shooting?

21:46

✷ Ella ✷
No, it's quiet. It's just the sirens, 5 times a day

Yeva Skalietska

21:48

Yeva
Dyana - For now at least.

22:38

Davyd
Where is everyone?

22:43

Kyrylo
I'm leaving for Poland

22:43

Kyrylo:
And I will be a Pole

22:59

Yeva
I'm happy for you

22:59

Yeva
Maybe we'll meet there

3 March 2022

FIRST CITY FALLS TO RUSSIANS

– Daily Telegraph

WELCOME TO HELL

– i

**PUTIN VOWS 'UNCOMPROMISING FIGHT'
AS UKRAINE WAR ENTERS SECOND WEEK**

– Kyiv Post

**MORE THAN 1M REFUGEES FLEE
UKRAINE IN FASTEST EXODUS
THIS CENTURY**

– Daily Telegraph

**IRELAND BACKS EU MOVE TO OFFER
SANCTUARY TO ALL UKRAINIANS**

– Irish Times

Day 8

Shocking News • On Our Way! • Beautiful Weeds •
Stopping and Starting

I woke up. I thought the night had been uneventful, but it turns out there had been some shelling somewhere far in the distance.

Granny got a text from one of her friends saying that her husband has been killed. He had gone to fetch some water from a spring and then – *BANG!* – a cluster bomb. The bomb fragments had cut his entire body. His leg got blown off. He was 47. He was a good man and a caring father. We spoke to him only a few days ago, and today he's gone. It's terrifying. We are in shock.

11 a.m. We needed to draw some cash and get some groceries. I offered to go.

When I got back, I learned that we're going to go to the train station to catch a train to Western Ukraine.

Our hosts called us a taxi and we didn't have to wait too long for it to come. We said our farewells. Inna is staying behind with her family. She told us that everything will be all right. We hope to see each other again. She also said that I should come back and finish my angel painting. Maybe I will, one day, after the war. We wished each other good luck. We got in the taxi and started talking to the driver – he told us he's from Donetsk.[29] We asked what the fare was and he said it was free. The people in this city are so nice.

Granny and I arrived at the train station. We went inside and tried to find out what do next, but no one seemed to know anything.

Suddenly, there was an announcement. 'Warning. Air raid. Take cover.' We rushed down into the subway connecting the platforms. While we were there, Granny asked a young lady what we should do. The lady was a volunteer called Rada. She said she could help us.

We found out that there was a train going to Truskavets (near Lviv) at 2 p.m., so we decided to try to catch it.

The air-raid siren eventually stopped and Rada took us to the waiting room. There were some other people there who we tried to talk to about what we'd been through, but they were locals, so it was hard for them to understand how bad things have been in Kharkiv.

We had some tea and biscuits. At 1 p.m., we thought we'd better start getting ready because the train would be arriving soon.

At last, our train's arrival was announced. We ran, along with a large crowd of others, towards the platform. We got out on to the platform and tried to make our way to our carriage. It wasn't easy, but we made it. Yay!

I was sitting on the window ledge, waiting for the train to start moving and for the crowd to shrink down as people filtered on. The train shook as it got going. The people left behind on the platform all started running somewhere else. They'd missed it. But we were on our way!

The conductor came by and told me to climb up to the top bunk, which I happily did. The trip was long but fun. I made friends with a girl called Lera, and we spent half the day laughing. She's from Kharkiv and we're the same age too, so we understand each other very well.

6 p.m. The sun is setting … I'm trying to imagine what it's like where we're going, but I can't.

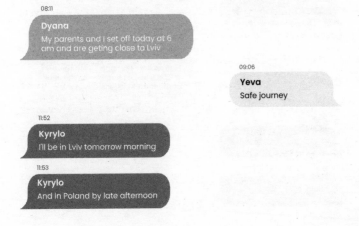

08:11

Dyana
My parents and I set off today at 6 am and are geting close to Lviv

09:06

Yeva
Safe journey

11:52

Kyrylo
I'll be in Lviv tomorrow morning

11:53

Kyrylo
And in Poland by late afternoon

13:12
✷ Ella ✷
OK

13:13
✷ Ella ✷
Good luck on the road 🍀

19:30
Nadya
I'm staying in Kharkiv

19:34
Polyna ☆
Our balcony windows smashed

19:37
☺ Myron☺
I've left

19:47
Nadya
We've been badly bombed

19:47
Nadya
So hard

19:47
Nadya
It's scary

19:47
Nadya
It's never been this loud

19:50
Yeva
Nadya, hold on, honey. Everything will be fine, just lie down on the floor, or maybe it's better to go to the basement

19:53
Nadya
My legs almost gave out

20:00
Polyna ☆
Better sit in the hallway

20:31
Andrey
What's up with school

20:31
Andrey
?

20:32
Polyna ☆
Looks like there's damage

20:32
Andrey
It might be on fire but I can't be sure

23:33
Polyna ☆
There's a siren in Lviv right now

It's dark outside. Lera was saying how beautiful the weeds out the window look, which really made me laugh. I suppose some people have to figure out where they're going and what to do next, but others might as well just admire the weeds. Ha!

There were some scary moments during our trip. The train kept slowing down and sometimes it stopped altogether. The lights in the carriage kept going out, and every time they came back on everyone would breathe a sigh of relief. There were times when I was too scared to speak. Later, Granny told me she'd seen explosions in the distance but she didn't tell me about them at the time because she didn't want to make me more frightened. I guess that's why the train was stopping – they were waiting for a signal that it was safe to keep going.

We passed by Kyiv. That was frightening too.

4 March 2022

'THEY'RE TRYING TO WIPE THIS CITY OFF THE FACE OF THE EARTH'

- Financial Times

PUTIN'S CHILLING WARNING: WORST IS YET TO COME

- Daily Telegraph

RUSSIAN ATTACK ON UKRAINIAN NUCLEAR POWER FACILITY ALARMS EXPERTS

- Irish Times

UKRAINE APPEALS TO RED CROSS TO ESTABLISH HUMANITARIAN CORRIDORS FOR BESIEGED CIVILIANS

- Kyiv Post

KREMLIN VOWS VICTORY IN UKRAINE AS REFUGEES SWELL TO ONE MILLION

- New York Times

Day 9

Where to Go? • It's Settled • What's in Store for Us? •
A Very Important Meeting

I woke up at six in the morning. We found out that the train is now terminating at Uzhhorod. I looked at the map and saw that Uzhhorod is in the far western end of Ukraine. At first, we thought we'd go there. But then we discovered that we could go to Romania or Germany from Lviv with my new friend Lera, and we thought, *Why not go with them?* But then we decided it would be more sensible to stay on the train, because if we changed at Lviv, we'd have to wait for three hours to get on a bus to the Romanian border and it was unclear what would happen once we got there. So, we settled on staying onboard until the end after all.

Lera and her mother got off the train in Lviv. We said goodbye, hoping we'd one day meet in Kharkiv. We're heading towards Uzhhorod, where there's a border with Slovakia and Hungary. We'll figure out the rest when we get there.

Passing a familiar site on the train – Mukachevo Castle.

On the train to Uzhhorod with my diary close to me.

8 a.m. A lot of people got off at Lviv, so our carriage is now half-empty. We move to a different compartment, where there is an empty bottom bunk.

A train conductor comes up to us. She's from Zaporizhzhia,[30] and she tells us that earlier the Russian occupiers seized the Zaporizhzhia nuclear power plant.[31] Its nuclear reactor is ten times more powerful than the one at Chernobyl. If it explodes, it will destroy everything in its path … and beyond.

1 p.m. It's been five hours – the trip is long and boring – and now we're in Mukachevo, in the west of the country. I can see Mukachevo Castle. I took a picture of it. I remember coming here last summer, but this time I'm trying to escape a war.

3 p.m. We eventually arrived in Uzhhorod, and the first thing we did was have something to eat at the station. Then, we went to the office that assigns accommodation. We were taken on to a bus. We didn't know where we were going. No one seems to know what's in store for us.

I'm realising that we've become refugees. Perhaps we will have the chance to go to the UK or Europe[32] and live there.

We arrived at the office for registration and placement. We were given a document with an address on it, and some volunteers drove us there in their car.

6 p.m. We've arrived at the address. It's a school. As we walked inside there was a man walking just behind us. He said hello in what I first thought was German, but then I realised he was actually speaking English. He wanted to ask me something, but I apologised and said I couldn't talk right now. I didn't know what was going on.

We were greeted by Myna. She's in charge here and she told us what's what. As she was showing us around the school, the man from before started filming us.

I don't know what to do with myself. I can feel the tension inside me; the stress of the situation is overwhelming. I have to find something to do. I need to figure out where I am, what I am, what is going on in the world. How am I supposed to sleep on a mattress in a school gym instead of my warm cosy bed? Where am I going to wash? There's no hot bath here.

I want to go back to school, *my* school, to my friends.

I feel numb.

8 p.m. While I was walking around, trying to occupy myself, Granny told the man who was filming us before that I am keeping a diary. How she managed that when he doesn't speak any Russian is a mystery to me … Still, that caught his attention. I went over and said hello. His name is Flavian. He works for Channel 4, a British TV channel.

I told him about everything that has happened to me. He asked if he could interview me about it on camera.

While they were looking for a room to film the interview

in, me and Flavian got talking and I learned that he's French. They couldn't find a room, so in the end we decided to talk right there in the middle of the school hall. During the interview, Flavian operated the camera, and I read him my diary. After that, Paraic, an Irish reporter working for *Channel 4 News*, asked me some questions.

We asked them if they could help us leave the country or find somewhere to live. They said they'd see if there was anything they could do. I'm hoping there is.

There are about fifty other people staying at this school gym.

10 p.m. I've been directed to my bed. I guess I'll try to sleep.

5 March 2022

NUCLEAR CATASTROPHE
'NARROWLY' AVERTED

– Guardian

RUSSIANS SEIZE EUROPE'S BIGGEST
NUCLEAR PLANT AND GAIN IN THE SOUTH
AS MORE UKRAINIANS FLEE

– New York Times

MORE AIR STRIKES REPORTED
ACROSS UKRAINE

– BBC

WAR IN UKRAINE WILL HAVE 'SEVERE IMPACT
ON THE GLOBAL ECONOMY', IMF WARNS

– CNN

UKRAINIAN ATHLETES OPEN THE
PARALYMPICS WITH SEVEN MEDALS

– Kyiv Post

Day 10

I Miss Kharkiv • Our Story • I Don't Feel Normal

I wasn't myself yesterday, but I've woken up feeling a bit better.

The situation in Kharkiv is very bad. It's hard to take in everything that's going on. The Ukrainian army asked some of our friends to leave the basement of their block of flats because it wasn't safe there. They were put on trucks. Where did they take them? No one knows. Down to the city centre, perhaps …

Half of Granny's friend's building has been demolished. All our friends still there want to leave Kharkiv. They've finally realised it's not safe. But it's harder to get out now.

I phone Olha. She's in Dnipro now. Apparently, it's all quiet there.

2 p.m. The reporters came back. I talked to them and then translated for Granny. We tell them our story of the first few days of the war.

Afterwards, we went down to the city centre for a look around.

Every building, every landmark, reminds me of Kharkiv. When I see the bridges overlooking this beautiful city, I think of Kharkiv and it pains my soul. Kharkiv is, or was, a lot prettier than Uzhhorod. But at least the chocolate here is good. We bought a new phone charger now that I can't borrow Inna's any more.

When we got back to the school, I felt miserable but I'm trying not to lose heart.

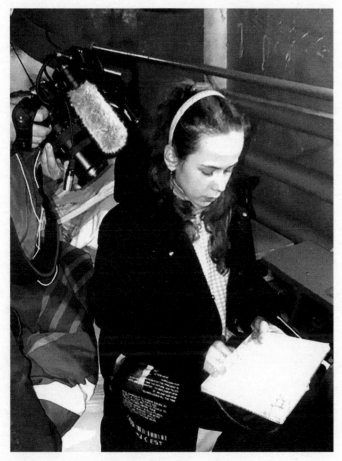

Reading my diary to the *Channel 4 News* team.

6 March 2022

**RUSSIA RESUMES SHELLING DURING
AGREED CEASEFIRE, HALTING
EVACUATION FOR SECOND DAY**

– Irish Times

**THOUSANDS JOIN PROTEST OVER
'BARBARISM' IN UKRAINE WAR**

– Independent

**MORE THAN 1.5 MILLION PEOPLE FLEE
UKRAINE WAR**

– Kyiv Post

**UKRAINE SUSPENDS EXPORTS OF SOME
PRODUCTS AS RISK OF FOOD
SHORTAGES GROWS**

– CNN

**'WE UNDERSTAND WHAT WAR MEANS':
POLES RUSH TO AID UKRAINE'S REFUGEES**

– Guardian

Day 11

It was an uneventful morning. We woke up, got ourselves sorted and went back down to the city centre for a walk. I'm falling in love with this city. I especially like the promenade along the Uzh River!

We were enjoying our day. I rang my school friend Khrystyna. We spent about thirty minutes chatting. Then I got a call from Freddie who is the *Channel 4 News* producer. They want to make a short film about us, so I sent them our location.

After a while, we met up with the reporters. We were filming something for *Channel 4 News* in the UK. They asked me to ring one of my friends. I thought I'd call Olha, but she wasn't picking up. However …

I had already spoken to Khrystyna today, so I thought to myself, *why not?* Why not record an interview with her? I asked

123

her mum for permission and then we started recording.

She is in Kharkiv. She's so fearless, being there. Khrystyna talked about what she does when there's shelling. She and her family all go to their hallway and wait it out. At times, I acted as a translator for her.

Once we were done filming, we went back to the school.

7 March 2022

'BARBARIC' PUTIN RAINS DOWN TERROR

- Daily Telegraph

FAMILIES FLEE FOR THEIR LIVES

- The Times

RUSSIA HITS UKRAINE FROM AIR, LAND
AND SEA WITH CIVILIANS TRAPPED

- Kyiv Post

RUN FOR YOUR LIVES

- Metro

'FALLING INTO EMPTINESS': UKRAINIAN
FAMILIES FEEL THE PAIN OF SEPARATION

- New York Times

Day 12

A New Acquaintance • Getting a New Passport
is Impossible

We've been talking about what we should do. We can't stay here because the school term will be starting soon and there's nowhere available to rent. We've decided we need to leave Ukraine altogether. But to do that, we need to get Granny a new passport because her old one was left back at our bombed flat.

We paid a visit to the Sovyne Hnizdo[33] (the registration centre). We were taken to the passport department, but it had been turned into a makeshift hospital for COVID patients. We met someone who helped us get through to the help hotline, but they told us they're not taking on any new cases until the end of the war. Yeah … so that's the situation – but we're determined we'll find a way into another country.

We went back to the town. Back in Dnipro, we had withdrawn quite a bit of cash from an ATM, but with no accommodation to spend it on we wanted to put it back into the bank. No such luck – the banks here aren't accepting Ukrainian currency for some reason, so we decided to exchange our hryvni into euros, but the rate isn't very good. I can buy one euro for forty-three hryvni, and sell one euro for thirty-eight hryvni. One euro used to cost about thirty hryvni, and the difference between buying and selling was never more than one hryvnia,[34] if that.

We returned to the school. The reporters introduced me to their colleague, Nik. She and her translator rang me, and we talked. I was telling her that I had no idea what we should do next. Should we stay in Ukraine or leave?

Before the phone call, an entertainer came to the school, dressed as a polar bear.

There was music and all the children danced.

A bit of entertainment at the refugee centre in Uzhhorod.

HUNGARY

8 March 2022

DAY BY DAY KHARKIV IS BECOMING MORE LIKE A GHOST CITY

– Kyiv Post

UKRAINE-RUSSIA TALKS MAKE LITTLE HEADWAY AS KYIV BRACES FOR ONSLAUGHT

– Irish Times

THE SICK CHILDREN FORCED FROM THEIR HOSPITAL BEDS BY PUTIN'S BOMBARDMENT

– Independent

MY HUSBAND STAYED TO FIGHT … WE'LL GO BACK TO KYIV WHEN WE HAVE VICTORY

– Evening Standard

THOUSANDS VOW TO HOUSE REFUGEES

– Irish Examiner

Day 13

We're Leaving • Our New Life Awaits • Farewell!

Today has been very eventful – I've had no time to write in my diary at all!

Soon after I woke up, we decided that we were definitely going to go to Hungary. Granny has heard that because of the situation sometimes the Hungarian authorities turn a blind eye if your papers aren't completely in order. Let's hope we get lucky.

We rang Father Emilio, a Catholic priest in Uzhhorod. We were given his contact details by the reporters. Father Emilio gave us the number for a volunteer. We then rang the volunteer who agreed that he would come and pick us up at the school and take us to Chop[35] near the Hungarian border. And, from there, we'll cross the border to Záhony.

'What time does the train leave?' we asked him.

'10:25 a.m.,' he replied.

'Will we get there on time?' It was in less than an hour.

He told us not to worry, it would only take us half an hour.

We got ready to leave. I ran back and forth around the school like a rocket, trying to gather up our things. We rang the volunteer again, and he said he'd be there in fifteen minutes.

Granny and I said goodbye to Myna and thanked her for the warm welcome. Our car arrived, and we introduced ourselves to the volunteer. His name is Arsenyi. He drove us all the way to the train station in Chop, and we shared our story with him. Around this time, I rang the TV reporters. They were waiting for us in Záhony.

We arrived in Chop at 10 a.m.. Arsenyi helped us find our way around the train station – he also helped us get our tickets. I was filming everything. We joined a large queue for border control. The train was late for some reason. We were supposed to leave at 10:25 a.m., but it was 12 p.m. by the time we were cleared to depart.

Granny and I presented our papers to the officials but … we needed one more document – a consent form for me to leave the country, signed by a parent, which we didn't have.

We'd had a serious row with Mum about this before she left for Turkey. There was already talk of war in Ukraine, but she was convinced that there wouldn't be an invasion. Getting that permit costs money, and she didn't want to spend hers on something she thought we wouldn't need.

We were kept back. They were trying to decide whether they could let us through into Hungary. We stood there, tears in our eyes, praying. *Please let us through.* And they did! They said that, even though we didn't have a consent document from Mum, and even though Granny didn't have her passport, they would let us through because normal rules don't apply during war time. They let us pass thanks to our prayers and our strong faith in God. I was overjoyed.

We got on to the train. Hurray! Granny found a seat and I stood up. After just twenty minutes, we were out of Ukraine and in Záhony – in Hungary! We waited for them to let us off the train. They were checking the passports of every single person on board. I was afraid they'd ask for that consent form again. Through the window, I saw the TV reporters on the platform. I waved at them, and they spotted me. When we were making our way slowly towards the train doors to get off, I saw Flavian casually climb down straight on to the tracks and start filming. That was funny.

After about forty-five minutes, it was finally our turn. They checked our papers and we got off the train. Thank goodness they didn't ask for the consent form.

We met up with the reporters and then were sent to the registration point. Unfortunately, the reporters weren't allowed in. Once Granny got her visa – valid for three months – we found them again. We immediately collected our train tickets, which some lady was handing out as if they were flyers, and then we all ran straight to the train headed for Budapest – the capital of Hungary.

All this time, my schoolmates were continuing to send messages in the school chat. Most people from my year at school are leaving Kharkiv now. Polyna fled to Germany, Maryna went to Kremenchuk in Central Ukraine and Kyrylo is at the Polish border.

No one speaks any English or Russian in Hungary. Maybe a few police and volunteers but, apart from that, it seems to be Hungarian-only. We're about to arrive in Budapest. At first, when I was looking at the city through the train window, it seemed ordinary and basic. I was quickly proven wrong … The train stopped at a platform just outside the station build-ing. We disembarked and I was shocked by what I saw. Keleti is a beautiful train station with giant columns propping up the enormous glass roof. The reporters began filming me. I went inside the main station building and there were statues along the walls. The volunteers were handing out anything you could ask for – things like shampoo, sanitary pads, nappies – we managed to get some toothpaste, toothbrushes and food.

I left the train station and had a look around. It was incredible! I won't stop saying it – what a beautiful city! A big shopping centre, old buildings, the commotion of people and cars all around me. I couldn't contain my emotions.

I'm in Europe! For the first time ever!

The reporters had sorted a lift for us so we went to find the car. We had to cross the road a few times and each time Granny and Paraic got stuck on the island in the middle of the road because they couldn't keep up. That was funny. We met Piotr, the driver, who is originally from Poland. We said our goodbyes to the reporters and agreed to meet up with them again tomorrow, then Piotr set off to take us to someone who has agreed to let us stay with them at their flat for a little while.

We drove to the other side of the city. Some of the streets and old temples here remind me of Kharkiv. We were approaching the Szechenyi Chain Bridge and it was beautiful. The view was enchanting; like something from a fairy tale – a boat floating, sparkling with bright lights all over it; street-lamps that give the river a romantic feel. There are incredible buildings on either side of the river: Buda Castle, the Hungarian Parliament and many other interesting things. I was speechless. I just kept thinking, *this is all so European!*

Piotr told us how the city got its name. According to him, Pest is named because of all the grocers there. And Buda is called that because it's the name of a castle on that side of the river.[36]

9 p.m. We've arrived and met our new host. His name is Attila and he was happy to see us. Attila showed us around our room, the shower and the kitchen and said that we were free to use all of them and that we'd talk more tomorrow. That's how nice he is. We think we've got a big day ahead of us tomorrow but, today, I'm about to drop from exhaustion.

9 March 2022

UKRAINE WAR AT 2-WEEK MARK: RUSSIANS SLOWED BUT NOT STOPPED

- Independent

NEARLY 35,000 PEOPLE RESCUED THROUGH HUMANITARIAN CORRIDORS, ZELENSKY SAYS

- CNN

ZELENSKY: NO-FLY ZONE NEEDED TO PREVENT HUMANITARIAN CATASTROPHE

- Kyiv Post

'BLOW TO PUTIN': BRITAIN AND US BAN RUSSIAN OIL

- Guardian

WE WILL *NEVER* SURRENDER

- Daily Mirror

Day 14

More New Acquaintances • Exploring Another City •
An Unforgettable Evening

I woke up at 8:30 a.m.. This is the first time I've slept through the entire night since the invasion. I dozed with a smile on my face, thinking of everything that happened yesterday.

I told Attila about what we've been through in Kharkiv and how we ended up here.

Today, we want to explore our new surroundings. And, by the way, we're staying almost in the city centre. The building we're in has a curious layout. The front door of the flat opens on to a long balcony overlooking a small courtyard.

Attila took a few pictures of us just now. He's a photographer.

The reporters introduced me to Delara and Tom – their colleagues from *Channel 4 News* – on the phone. We're going to meet up. I can't wait!

Time passed. I walked around the flat impatiently, looking forward to meeting them. And then, someone rang the buzzer. It was them. I hurried to let them in and immediately got lost! Eventually, after a few minutes, I found the front door. We introduced ourselves and I took them up to the flat. We started talking and I told them my story, starting from the very beginning. After a while, we were joined by the other *Channel 4 News* reporters. I went to let them in – I didn't get lost this time – then recorded an interview. They are all are going on to Moldova, but we're staying here with Delara and Tom. Oh well … Pity. I wished them a safe journey. I'm really going to miss them.

After they left, Granny and I decided to go for a walk down by the river. I grabbed a map and we set off. However, we weren't quite sure how to get there. We asked a Hungarian girl but she spoke very little English. I explained everything to her using a translator app and she gave us directions, but we could barely understand her. Then, as we kept walking, we asked some other people, but they didn't even look our way. This is some kind of discrimination!

We went for a wander around the park next to our flat instead. After our walk, we wanted to find a chemist. Thank God we met another girl who spoke English. She took us to the chemist, but it turned out to be a medical laboratory. She tried giving us new directions, but we couldn't really make sense of them. I forgot to say that the sirens on ambulances, fire trucks and police cars here in Budapest are very loud. You could turn it down a little!

That's when I got a call from Delara inviting us on river-boat tour to do some sightseeing. We were delighted! We didn't hesitate to accept. They'll be picking us up at 7:45 p.m., and we'll go on a boat to get a better look at Budapest.

7:46 p.m. The doorbell rang and I ran to open it, tripping over myself in my excitement. We got into a taxi and drove through the city centre, then waited to get on the boat.

After a while, we began boarding. I eagerly stepped onto the boat and we made our way to the top deck. The boat started moving. We were going down the river. I stepped outside from the indoor passenger deck to get some air and saw we were passing by the Hungarian Parliament Building. It's so beautiful. I've never seen the American White House, but I'm confident that the Hungarian Parliament Building is a million times prettier. It's unbelievably big, like a palace. The Hungarian flag on its roof really stands out, and the building is illuminated at night which gives it a romantic feel. Then we passed under bridges, admired the castle, saw the city in all its glory. I stood there, shocked by all this beauty. We filmed an interview during our river tour. I was about to burst from all the emotions I was feeling. Then the boat turned around. I enjoyed every moment of it.

We docked and returned to the flat. I thanked Tom and Delara for a beautiful evening. I was so tired that when we got back to the flat, I collapsed into bed and fell into a deep sleep.

A wonderful night in Budapest, on a boat on the River Danube
with the *Channel 4 News* crew.

10 March 2022

'GENOCIDE': RUSSIA BOMBS UKRAINE CHILDREN'S HOSPITAL

- Guardian

THEY BOIL SNOW FOR WATER, WITH DEATH IN THE AIR

- New York Times

'NO PROGRESS' AFTER RUSSIAN, UKRAINIAN FOREIGN MINISTERS MEET FOR 1ST TALKS SINCE INVASION

- The Week

UKRAINE CRISIS ADDS TO FEARS OVER WORLD FOOD PRODUCTION

- Scotsman

MAYOR KLITSCHKO: HALF OF KYIV POPULATION FLED

- Kyiv Post

Day 15

A Walk in a Budapest Park • Meeting New People

During the night some refugees from Odessa[37] came to the flat and stayed over. And earlier on today some other refugees arrived.

We're going to meet Delara and Tom later and I'm going to read them my diary. I can't wait to see them. The rest of the *Channel 4 News* crew are in Moldova now.

We decided to go for a walk and both Granny and I felt a little more confident this time. We took a stroll around the park. Today has been a warm and sunny day.

After our walk, we returned to the flat and Tom and Delara came by to film me reading from my diary.

Every day, I text and call my friends. I ask them what the situation in Kharkiv is. I talk to my Granny Zyna and Grandad Yosip who are still there.

Tomorrow is a big day. I've been keeping a secret from this diary ever since we met the reporters. Tomorrow, everything shall be revealed …

IRELAND

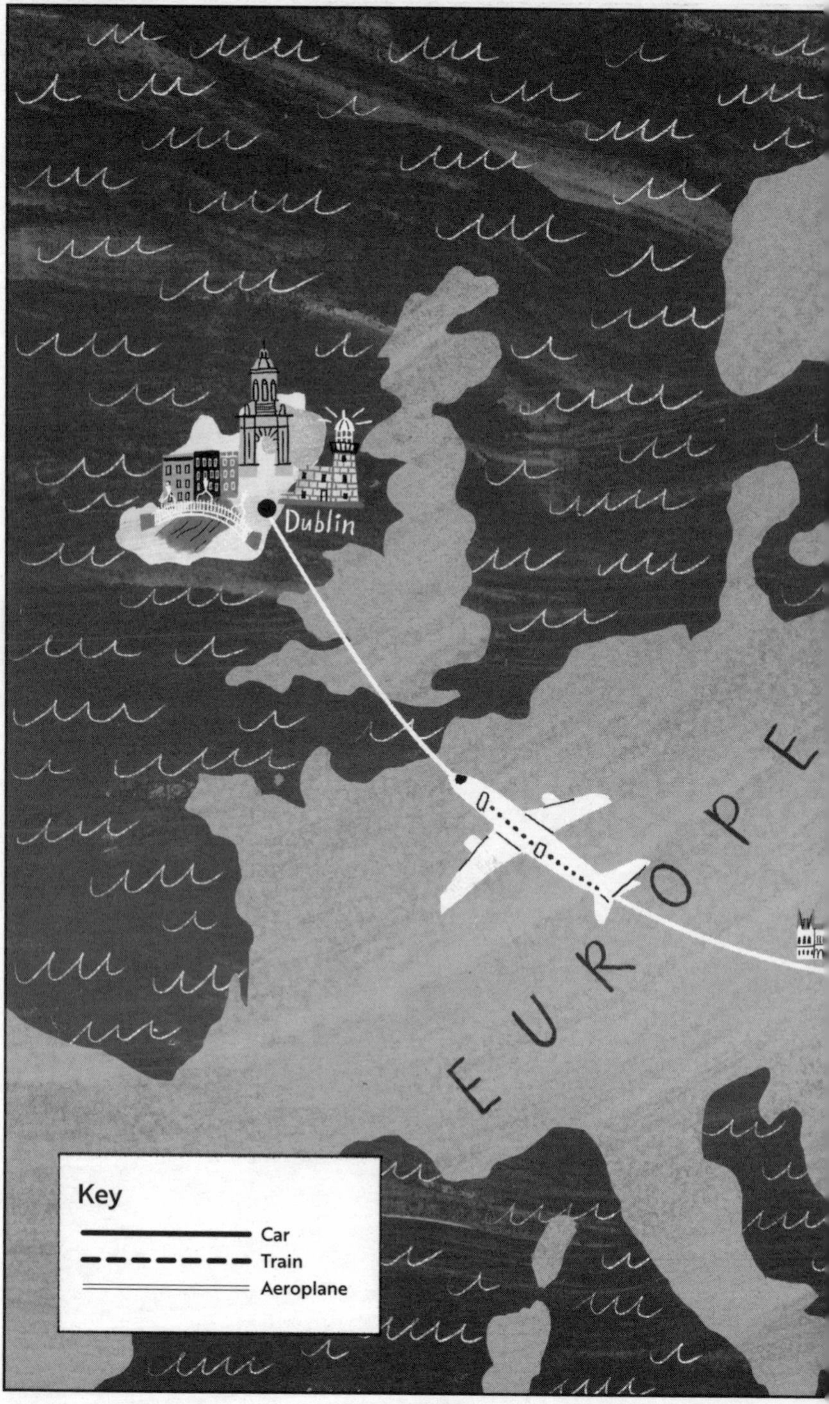

Dublin

EUROPE

Key

——— Car
- - - Train
=== Aeroplane

OUR
JOURNEY

UKRAINE

Kyiv

Kharkiv

Lviv

Dnipro

Uzhhorod
Chop
Záhony

Budapest
JNGARY

Sochi

Day 16

I'm Flying Away • The Ruse is Up •
Someone Is Expecting Us

Today, I'm leaving for Dublin, Ireland. I've been keeping that fact from this diary for ages! So, let me explain. Since the very first day I met them, I've been asking the reporters to help us get to England. After about three days, it became clear that in order to do so, we'd need to have family there. They said we could go to Ireland or France instead. We'd heard that the people of France aren't very welcoming towards immigrants, and we don't speak any French. So, we decided to go to Ireland.

During our phone conversation, Nik explained the process and sent us a document. The reporters were helping us along the way, and it was no accident that we ended up in Budapest. We got our plane tickets yesterday – Tom and Delara showed them to us on their phones.

We decided to go for a walk in the park and then go to a

shopping centre. We met up with Tom and Delara there, and we sat down at a café and talked. At first, they said they'd come with us to Ireland, but then they said they couldn't after all. They walked us back to the flat and we began packing. Then, we sat down for the road[38] before we set off to the airport.

We arrived and went inside. Everything was sorted for us, and we got handed our tickets. Once we reached the security check, we said our farewells to Tom and Delara and they told us to reach out to them if we needed help with anything. We went through security and ended up in the departure lounge. We sat around, waiting for our gate number to be announced.

An hour went by. The gate number appeared on the screen – B24. We made our way to border control. Once through, we located our gate. All we had to do now was wait.

Our flight was delayed. We were supposed to depart at 8:20 p.m..

We stood in a queue for half an hour. Finally, it started moving. Staff checked our boarding passes and asked us to put our masks on. I searched through my pockets. No mask – no flight. There might be a war happening, but COVID hasn't gone anywhere. I was beginning to worry that this one tiny thing could mean us missing our plane. But, thank God, it was all sorted. The flight attendant gave us some masks just as I was about to give in to despair. The queue began slowly moving along on to the plane.

We spent a lot of time waiting for the aeroplane to take off. Finally, it started moving. I picked up my phone and began filming. The aeroplane picked up speed as it travelled down the runway, and finally we took off! It was awesome! I felt so happy, because I was going to a safe country and because there were people waiting to meet us at the airport.

I had phoned the people who are going to host us in Dublin – Catherine and her husband, Gary – before take-off. They would meet us at the airport. The flight took two hours and forty minutes. I couldn't wait for us to get there.

Finally, the plane landed. We had arrived in Dublin! I turned my phone off flight mode and saw that it was bursting with messages. I wanted to reply to them all, but I wasn't connected to the internet.

We left the aeroplane and walked through many long corridors. It felt like we were going in circles to get to border control. Once there, there was a problem with Granny's papers, but it all got sorted and she was given a visa allowing her to stay for ninety days. We'll sort the rest later. For now, we were just trying to find our way out of the airport because someone was waiting for us ...

We asked for directions to the exit. We walked through the doors and ... there was a crowd of people awaiting our arrival. There were television reporters, our hosts' friends and family and our hosts themselves – Catherine and Gary. It was a warm welcome. We kept hugging each other.

I'm very happy.

11 p.m. Now we're going to go find the car and head to the house. The Irish are very kind and friendly. By the way, they drive on the left side of the road here.

3 a.m. When we got into the car, I rang the *Channel 4 News* crew and thanked them for all their help laying out this path for us, for the wonderful hosts they found and for making us feel safe.

We arrived very late, at midnight. There's a dog at the house called Buddy. I gave him some cuddles. We were shown around the house and to our room. I was showered with gifts – a new set of pyjamas, toiletries, some comfy clothes and toys. I'm writing this now because I'm so excited that I can't sleep!

A warm welcome at Dublin airport – me, Catherine and Granny.

Making a new friend in Dublin!

12 March 2022

Day 17

Warm Welcomes • Feeling Positive

Today a brand new day in a brand new country is waiting for me. I met our new neighbours and they welcomed me warmly to Ireland. We hugged. They were so happy to see us. Even though Granny doesn't speak any English, she could see how sincere these people were. Some brought flowers. Others brought gifts. It was such a lovely feeling.

We sat and talked. They were very interested in our story. Then one of the neighbours asked if I wanted to go over to her house to play their piano. I was glad to, but hadn't played anything in almost a month. At first, I struggled to remember how to play any of the music I'd learned, but soon it all came flooding back to me. Hearing the sound of a piano again felt wonderful. It was such a joy to play some classical music.

7 p.m. In the evening, more neighbours came by, and they had a daughter my age. Her name was Nina. She asked if I wanted to go and do some baking with her. I really love baking all sorts of tasty things, so I said yes! We had fun talking as we mixed the ingredients. Together, we put the scones in the oven and then went to play a board game with her mum, which was a lot of fun. I was very pleased because I won.

Once we were done playing, it was time to take the scones out of the oven. They were pretty. And then I needed to get back to Catherine and Gary's house. What a fun evening! I brought some of the scones to share and everyone liked them. They were just so yummy!

Finally, I'm playing music again.

Day 18

The Interview • A Visit to a Ukrainian
Catholic Church • The Irish Sea

This morning, some Irish reporters filmed an interview with me which is going to be on the TV this evening. It will be the first time I've seen myself on TV but I don't really feel very excited about it. Inside, I'm just thinking of my home. Inside I'm in pain.

After that, we went to a Ukrainian Catholic church to attend Mass. We prayed for ourselves and for everyone we love back in Kharkiv.

Gary came to fetch us, and I was pleased to see he had Buddy in the car with him. He asked if we wanted to go for a walk along the beach by the Irish Sea. We jumped at the chance!

When we arrived, I could feel the wind on my face and blowing through my hair. We climbed down to the sand and it was low tide, which made the beach look huge. I took some pictures. The sea was breathtakingly beautiful. I was all wrapped up in a snug, warm coat but the kite-surfers there were rushing bravely into the water, not minding the cold one bit! They were fascinating to watch, gliding over the waves. The sea was like a mirror, reflecting the sky. I ran around on the sandy beach enjoying every wonderful moment. I felt overwhelmed with emotion. Buddy was zooming around too, and I kept trying to catch him. It was so thrilling.

Then, we went to take a look around the city. Trees are planted along the banks of the river. Gorgeous green parks that you can actually run around in, not like the lawns in Kharkiv!

When we got home the pupper[39] was completely spent. It was a truly beautiful day.

Day 20

News from Kharkiv • Gary's School • The EPIC Museum • The Book of Kells

Yesterday, we phoned my other grandparents, Granny Zyna and Grandad Yosip. They told us they'd moved basements and are currently holed up underground somewhere on Haharina Avenue in the south of Kharkiv. It's a far more comfortable set up, with spaces to sleep, wash-up, cook and eat. I felt relieved for them, because their last basement was a very unpleasant damp place.

Marfa, Granny's friend, went to fetch some bread and met some volunteers working from a tent to give people aid. The next day, when she left the basement again, she saw that the tent had gone – all that was left was rubble.

8 a.m. Catherine and Gary are both teachers. Today, I visited Gary's school. I met the other girls there – they were older than me but we still had fun together.

The entire group then left the school to go on a school trip. We got on a train. I could see Dublin through the window. The curious thing about Dublin is that there aren't any buildings taller than five storeys here. European-style streets. Stunning red-brick buildings. It surprised me that the city doesn't have a metro!

We walked over a bridge that straddles the River Liffey – it's amazing. I'm looking around and seeing many different bridges. They each have something special about them. Some of them are tall, large and are built to allow cars to drive over them. But others are small, for pedestrians only. We walked along Dublin's best-known street – Grafton Street. We walked by the river, and made a turn towards EPIC, The Irish Emigration Museum.

We kept together, like a row of geese.

Then, we entered the glass building of the EPIC Museum. We got our 'museum passports' – fun little booklets with a map of the museum's exhibits which you can mark off with a stamp as you visit them. We went inside. There was a lot of information about the history of Ireland to take in and I couldn't always understand everything. There were videos projected on to the walls. We learned about the history of the courts, the famine, the wars, national holidays and Irish food and dance. I tried doing some of the moves. I don't mean to brag, but I think I was actually quite good at it!

After the museum, we made our way to Trinity College.

On the way, I was amazed by how pretty all the streets and shops looked. And then we stepped inside the library and saw the ancient Book of Kells.[40] It's very big, 1200 years old and written in Latin. We weren't allowed to take photos. Then, we walked up some stairs and entered a very long library. Two stories filled with books. I had no doubt you could find a few of Pushkin's poems there (that's whose name popped into my head when I tried to think of a writer, I don't know why). Someone played the theme music from Harry Potter on their phone and, straight away, I imagined I was at Hogwarts.

On our way back to the train, I saw a beautiful bus – sort of like the ones they have in London, but more colourful. When I finally arrived back at the house, I was so tired I could barely put one foot in front of the other. I crashed out with Buddy cuddled up on top of me. Happy, I fell into a deep sleep.

Day 21

Catherine's School • Irish Dancing •
Svyatohirs'k Destroyed

I'm enjoying being here but today I was overcome by sadness. I miss home, I miss my friends, I miss my school.

Catherine took me into the school where she teaches. My sadness gradually disappeared and I had another try at Irish dancing with the girls there. The school lessons were fun. During playtime, we went out on to the green courtyard. I tried reading a book in English at the library but I had quite a bit of trouble and couldn't understand much, so I had to use the translator app. I need to improve my English. I'm not too worried though, I'll learn.

I had a wonderful day in Dublin, but it was a horrible day in Kharkiv and in the Donetsk Oblast.

There used to be a huge shopping centre next my school, but not anymore – it has been destroyed. There's a rumour that the Russian army are going to start using chemical weapons[41] against remaining survivors. It's basically genocide against the Ukrainian people at this point!

There's a famous city in Ukraine called Svyatohirs'k. It has a beautiful monastery. I visited there just last summer, relaxing and enjoying life, and today it was bombed. Destroyed.

Day 22

*The British Reporters Come for a Visit •
My First St. Patrick's Day*

Today, our friends, the Channel 4 reporters, are going come to Dublin because it's St. Patrick's Day. I was delighted! We're going to go see the parade and we have to wear something green.

Catherine and I are making cupcakes with green icing. I tried the frosting mix and ... my teeth turned green! I spent five minutes trying to decide whether or not to brush them again. I was still thinking about it when I heard the doorbell. That was very awkward.

But I quickly brushed my teeth and they were white again. Phew!

I came out into the hallway and saw that Paraic and the crew were there. We hugged. I'd missed them.

When we got to the parade, the reporters began filming. I made my way through a small crowd to get a better look. There were so many different people. Soldiers, musicians, acrobats – anyone you could think of. There were also people dressed as characters from Irish history and folklore, but we didn't know who any of them were … yet. I watched with delight, so excited to see who would come round the corner next.

The parade was almost over and we were getting ready to leave, but Paraic was nowhere to be seen. We set off together to search for him. Just as I was beginning to feel that we'd searched through half the city centre, Paraic finally turned up.

Then we saw a couple wrapped up in Ukrainian flags. We talked to them. Turns out, they'd only arrived in Dublin a couple of days ago.

The main thing I wanted to know was, 'Were there lots of aeroplanes in the sky where you were? How did you cope with the terrible noise?'

They said, 'On the very first day, as we ran, we saw aeroplanes fly over our heads. After that, we moved countries five times before deciding to come to Dublin.'

It wasn't a long conversation, but everything came back to me: the good and the bad. I felt sadness and pain. Tears welled up in my eyes. I remembered how I cried as I prayed for my home to be spared from the bombs. I thought of Kharkiv and all the important things in it which have now been destroyed.

When I got into the taxi to go home, tears started rolling down my face.

Me having fun at the St. Patrick's Day Parade in Dublin.

18 March 2022

18 March 2022

**TWELVE-YEAR-OLD UKRAINIAN YEVA
IS ONE OF MILLIONS WHO HAVE BEEN
FORCED TO FLEE THE COUNTRY AFTER
RUSSIA'S INVASION. SHE'S BEEN KEEPING
A DIARY OF THE LONG JOURNEY THAT
HAS NOW SAFELY ENDED IN IRELAND.**

– Channel 4 Twitter feed

Day 23

Fun at the Zoo • A Lot to Take In

Today, we went to the zoo. I was excited. I was very interested to see what the zoo in Dublin is like.

We got in the car and drove to a large park. It had green open spaces and small thickets. I wanted to get out of the car and run around on the grass. The park was so vast that it would take an entire day to explore it all. The president of Ireland has a house somewhere in these grounds, but we didn't go to it.

The park was great, but that was just the tip of the iceberg. The zoo was incredible! The lemurs jumped around in the trees, like they never even suspected they were living in a zoo. They were all different colours: there were red ones and grey ones and black ones too. The tiger was teasing everyone by hiding behind some trees, forcing everyone to wait around for it to come out. Meanwhile, the lions were laying out in the sun, without a care in the world. The sea lions kept popping their heads out of the water, before diving back down again. There were about seven giraffes huddled together, trying to nudge their way to some leaves. The gorillas were hanging out on their island, deep in conversation. We nearly got lost in a bamboo grove on our way to the elephant enclosure. I couldn't get over how huge the rhinoceroses were.

We were about halfway through the route when it got *really* pretty. There was an artificial waterfall that glistened in the sun. There was a lake, surrounded by a small jungle with monkeys jumping from tree-to-tree. A small bridge took us over the lake and on to a little island. I wanted to climb over the railing and go and play with the monkeys on their island but I was becoming really tired so I couldn't, even if it was allowed! It was getting harder to walk. I was enjoying the zoo, but I hadn't any energy left. We didn't have time to see everything, but the things we did see were incredible.

With each day, Dublin is getting more and more interesting. More and more amazing.

Day 25

Each Day Weighs Heavier on My Soul •
The Horrors Keep Coming • The Castle and the Field •
The Sea and Rocks of Gary's Childhood

I want to dedicate today's diary entry to my friends and family who are still back home. Our friend, Marfa, has told us that it is painful to talk about what has become of Kharkiv.

She says a block of flats next to the hospital was on fire. The district heating offices have been wiped off the face of the Earth.

Granny's friend Anzhela sent us a video of the kindergarten near our flat – it's been bombed. No one would have been inside but I hope the flat itself is all right.

Our neighbour fled to Germany with her mother. Granny's friend Nelya fled to Poland along with her son. My grandparents are still holed up in the basement on Haharina Avenue in Kharkiv. My aunt and uncle are in Poltava, together with my cousin.

We rang Motrona. She works at a funeral home and said she

was in the middle of a funeral procession when shelling started up. She's afraid for her life.

Over the last few days, we've become real tourists. Today we went to Malahide Castle and a beautiful beach.

We visited a park on the way. The blue sky was full of different shades and the white clouds lay flat across it, just like they do in a painting. The green lawn was perfectly cut. It was so pretty that I instantly felt the urge to go run around on it. The whole place had a smell of freedom.

We parked the car and headed towards a tall pine forest. Then, we made our way to the castle. I caught a glimpse of one of its towers in the distance. It looked like something from medieval times. We turned a corner and Malahide Castle appeared before us in all its glory. It was built in the 12th century, but it still looks stunning. I turned round and saw a wide clearing behind us. I ran, holding on to Buddy's lead. The poor little guy kept tripping over himself as he struggled to keep up. I lay down on the grass and put my arms around him. I felt free.

Gary thought we could go to a place called Portmarnock Beach next, near where he grew up.

There, sky-blue water and sandbars stretched out into the distance. There were people there taking a stroll, and it seemed to me like they were walking over the sky.

We climbed down some steps. The tide was out. There were little rock pools reflecting the sunlight, making it look as if they

Me and the Irish Sea.

were covered in ice.

The sun was going down, and the sky was incredibly beautiful. The waves slammed against the rocks. There was a breeze coming from the sea. I thought I'd have an adventure and climb the rocks. They were slippery. Just as I was getting confident, Granny called to me to get back down to take a photo. I was very disappointed because I'd gone through all that trouble to climb across, and it was all in vain. I took in the splendid horizon. The blue of the water, the sky painted pinkish-purple and blueish-white. It was magnificent. I couldn't stop looking at it, but it was time to go back.

All of that was wonderful and beautiful but, every night before bed, we watch the news about Ukraine and Kharkiv. The shelling continues. The Grads and missiles make us feel desperate. My family is hiding in a shelter. It's horrible and frightening to think about.

Day 26

Yeva 20:17
Are you in Ukraine?

Evhen 20:17
Yes

Fylymon 20:17
Me too

Evhen 20:17
Near the border

Fylymon 20:18
Somewhere in the Cherkasy region

Yeva 20:28
And I'm abroad

Yeva 20:28
A long way from war

Fylymon 20:32
Will you ever come back

Yeva 20:32
I feel great here

Fylymon 20:33
Where are you

Yeva 20:33
Far far away

Day 28

A Cry of the Soul • Pain for Kharkiv

The war has been going on for a month now. It has brought so much suffering to my friends and my family – to everyone. How many lives has this war taken already, and how many more is it yet to claim? No one knows what will happen tomorrow, or in an hour, or even in a minute …

The fewer people who know what war is, the better. The world would be a happier place because there's nothing worse than war.

Every day, my heart gets torn to pieces as I watch what's happening in my home country, in my home town. Those who survive the war will never be the same as before. They will enjoy life and enjoy their days again but only because it's a day without war.

Now they know, and will forever know, what it's like to wake up to the sounds of shelling and missiles. And what it's like to pray for their home every day. Today, your home wasn't hit by a missile, but tomorrow things might be different.

Every day, there are more and more blocks of flats being bombed. And I'm growing more and more tired of asking *Why are you fighting? Who's going to rebuild all of this and how long will that take? Why did you need to start this?* We were living in peace and harmony!

What pains me most is how many innocent civilians and children are getting killed. The Russian army are ruthlessly launching their bombs, wiping cities off the face of the Earth.

What is left of my home. I feel such sorrow when I think of Kharkiv.

Day 33

The Letter • Gratitude

The time has come for our reporters to move on to other stories. *The Channel 4 News* crew sent me an email which said that we won't be hearing from them for the foreseeable future. There are times when they focus on stories about specific people, but there are also times when they must work on other important assignments. It's reassuring for them to know that we are in a safe country now. The fact that they must now focus on other things might be difficult for everyone to accept, because it might seem like they're moving on and leaving behind those they've met along the way. But that couldn't be further from the truth. They shall never forget us … and we shall never forget them. I hope that we shall remain friends forever … I sent them a letter, in English:

Dear Paraic and all the team at Channel 4 News,

You are the kindest people who we could have met in our lives. You changed our lives for the better, and I don't know what would have happened if we had not met you. You rescued us from the war and saved our lives. This was a great deed and not many people would have done this in the same situation. Any problems that we have now, I think, will be solved and everything will be great. Also, I want to say thank you for your help in finding a good literary agent. Maybe I will meet her soon and my diary will find its own publisher (I never dreamed this would happen before I met you). I believe we will stay friends forever and ever (even if we don't keep in touch with each other often). I really hope we will meet again someday. I send you lots of good wishes. Thank you seems like too small a word to say for everything you have done for us.

Yeva and Iryna

Paraic visited Kharkiv and sent us this photo of a rocket lodged in a crater by my block of flats.

Day 34

Howth • The Lighthouse

Today we went on a trip that has changed everything I thought I knew about travelling. I saw some palm trees today and for a few seconds, I was transported back to Sochi[42] where my great-grandma lives. It was odd to see those trees – it was like there was a bit of Sochi here with me. I used to spend entire summers there, splashing around in the sea. But now the war has divided Russia and Ukraine. It's so sad. It hurts to know that I have been separated from my family. I want so badly for all of this to be over and for there to be peace between Russia and Ukraine. I want to visit my great-grandma.

Later, we followed a winding road all the way to the very top of Howth Summit. We got out of the car and a beautiful view of the sea opened up before us. We made our way down a path and saw a lighthouse at the very edge of the coast. It was surrounded by cliffs, relentlessly battered by the surf. The waves raced each other, triumphantly crashing against the rocks. And the lighthouse stood there, quietly watching over the ships. The ships went by, one after another. The weather was amazing, not a cloud in the sky. If you took a boat straight from here, you could reach Wales. At the water's edge, it seemed liked there was no end to the sea. A boundless horizon. I sat down on a warm little boulder and looked out ... Such sorrow ...

Day 37

First Day at School • New Teachers and Schoolmates • Missing My Old School

Today was my first proper day at an Irish school. I was excited. I pulled on my new teal school uniform as soon as I woke up. We got in the car and drove all the way across Dublin to get to the school. There was a lot of traffic, but as we drove over the bridge I felt excited to be a part of it all. Little cars going about their business like bees in a hive. And the sun was calling for everyone to get out of bed. The city was coming alive.

School started at 8:30 a.m.. Phew! I made it on time. My new classmates welcomed me and were all very friendly. I attended each lesson eagerly, my face glued to the translator app. I had to switch from what I had been learning at my Ukrainian school to the Irish curriculum – and do it all in a different language too. It's an all-girls school and I made friends with some of them. It was all very exciting. Everything's in English.

Me in my new school uniform.

There are grand pianos here that I can play music on. New teachers. Green tennis courts. A huge library. And the school grounds are beautifully kept. Awesome!

My new friends and teachers were all nice, but I missed my old ones. The war has forced us all to scatter across the globe.

People are fleeing Kharkiv every day. Our friend Marfa is no exception. Since the start of the war, she and her family kept having to move from one basement to another. Like the tin soldier,[43] they held on for as long as they could, not wanting to leave home. Every day, they hoped for all this to be over soon. But everything changed in an instant. A missile hit very near where they were staying, killing a child and scattering dead bodies all over the neighbourhood. Now they know they have to flee. They're looking for a team of volunteers to help get their large family (seven people) out of Kharkiv and into Dnipro.

I can't stand the word 'refugee'. I never could. When Granny began referring to us as refugees, I immediately asked her to stop doing that. Inside, it made me feel ashamed. I've only just understood why. I'm ashamed to admit that I don't have a home … It's felt unbearable ever since we fled our flat to go to the basement. My dream is that someday soon we'll have our own place again.

Day 61

*Our Things Have Been Moved • My Cat Chupapelya
is Safe • The State of Our Flat*

Things are finally easing a little bit, after almost two whole months of war! This whole time, our flat has been standing there, bombed from two sides, with its windows shattered and the door blasted off. The worst part is, the shelling continued even during the Orthodox Easter celebrations.[44] They have no shame! It is just too hard to bear!

When we finally realised that we should start getting what remained of our things out of the flat, we asked around to try and find someone who could move our things from that dangerous place.

Eventually, Granny was given the number for a person called Trofym who could help us. He said he'd pick up anything we asked him to, even the chandelier, no problem. He had already moved out entire shops, cars and flats. All we had to do was tell him where to go to pick the stuff up from and where to drop it off, and he would go there first thing (provided there wasn't too much shelling) and grab everything he could.

When we fled our flat I had no time to pack my oil paints (a New Year[45] present from Grandad), my favourite clothes and, most importantly, my beautiful pink toy cat Chupapelya!

Granny made a list of all the things she wanted to be rescued from the flat and where to find them. She included my oil paints, but she said that Chupapelya would be just fine. I was sad, but I hoped that he would rescue her anyway and take her to Granny's friend's place, along with the rest of our things. We agreed that early tomorrow morning he would go and pick up our things.

But in the meantime, today he went to find our friend's car, to make sure that it was still in one piece and hadn't been stolen. He also dropped by both ours and our friend's flats to see what state they were in.

First, he checked on our friend's car. It was still where she left it. Its windows were shattered (from a blast wave), and the doors and boot were slightly damaged. The front of the car, along with the bonnet, was fine which meant that it was fit to drive, or it would have been had it not been for the fact that the battery had been stolen.

After that, he went to our flat, and it was painful to look at, even though we were only looking at a photo on a phone screen. Trofym unsealed the tape attaching our front door in

The terrible destruction inside my flat. This is the hallway. You can see Granny's German fridge on the floor. Months later, Trofym went back to our flat again and found an unexploded munition right there, underneath the fridge. He ran for his life. Thank God he was okay.

What is left of the entrance to my flat.

place and lifted it out the way. Inside, the hallway, as I've mentioned before, was buried under heaps of debris and lying on the floor was our expensive German fridge and the wall was caved in. The wardrobe by the front door was blown to bits. Clothes everywhere. The bedroom windows were shattered, the flowerpots were thrown off the windowsill. Lying on the bed was my toy cat Chupapelya. By some miracle, she had been spared. The television in the living room was damaged. The sofa facing the hallway was also hit (quite badly). But, our armchair, which stood right next to the hallway, was untouched. The living room was covered in a thick layer of dust.

Trofym will go to the flat to collect our things at 6:30 a.m. Ukrainian time. I set Granny's alarm for 4:30 a.m. and we both went to bed.

7:30 a.m. I was getting ready for school when Granny shared some good news. Trofym moved all of our surviving posses-sions – he even managed to get the two-metre wide chandelier from the hallway by cutting it from the ceiling – and brought everything over to our friend, Motrona. Most importantly, he also brought my oil paints and Chupapelya. Now she is safe with Motrona!

My joy knew no bounds. We will never be able to repay that man – words can't describe how grateful we are! Such a weight off my shoulders …

Day 67

*A New Little House • Our Beautiful Dacha
in Vovchansk*

We've been offered a house to rent! It's a small place near my
new school in South County Dublin. It might not belong to us,
but we don't mind.

We went to have a look at it. It turned out to be a cosy
little house with a garden. The best part is that it's only a five
minute walk from my new school. We were met by two kind
women, Linda and Juliette. They showed us around. There are
flowers everywhere.

We have a dacha[46] in Vovchansk, north-east of Kharkiv,
it's a big, beautiful house. There are a lot of orchard trees
there, and loads of flowers there too. There's a river nearby –
Siverskyi Donets. I loved taking my shoes off and going
down for a swim among the blooming white waterlilies there.

Then in the evening, Granny and I would sit by the big fireplace and drink tea. In the autumn, I'd go for a walk in the tall pine and oak forest and forage for mushrooms. There were loads of different kinds! Butter mushrooms, penny buns, bay boletes and chanterelles.[47]

That's all great, but the Russian occupiers are there now. It's so sad.

We are grateful to the kind Irish people who have helped us find a new house.

Afterword

This concludes this part of my diary. I don't know how many more days, months, or even years this war is going to last for. How many lives it will claim, how much heartbreak it will cause, how big a toll it will take – and has already – remains to be seen. To this day, there are people suffering in Kharkiv, and I am amazed that they have the strength and will to carry on. Since this war began, I have learned to truly value my life. Sooner or later, everyone gets to learn that lesson.

I've dreamed about the first day of the war many times. In it, I am about leave, to go somewhere safe, and, with tears streaming down my face, I tell my classmates that we shall never see each other again.

In one terrible instant, life has turned upside down and taken a totally different direction. Before the war, life had its problems, but it was still good. I remember rushing to get to school with my classmates. I remember trying to look pretty for the older boys. It was all as it should be. One day, I'm worn out from bowling at my birthday party. The next, I'm worn out from having to dive down into the basement time and time again; exhausted from the fear that every day of this war brings.

Perhaps, in many years' time, I shall see my classmates and family again. But, for now, I am turning over a new leaf, and I'm making new friends and meeting new classmates. The most important thing I want to say is that I believe only a strong faith in God can bring miracles.

My Friends' Stories

When the war began, my friends and I were all forced down separate paths. Each of us experienced different situations and moments where we really needed each other's support. Some of us fled the city on the very first day, some held on until the very last second, and others are still in Kharkiv even as I write this. I gave some of my friends the opportunity to be included in my book and they jumped at the chance! I asked them to write about their experiences, as well as their hopes and wishes for the future.

Khrystyna's Story

24 February 2022, 4:50 a.m. – I shall remember the date and time forever. The terrified look in my mother's eyes and the confused tone of her voice as she kept saying, 'Wake up,

children. Get dressed, quickly now, come on …'

I didn't hear the first explosion, but I heard the ones that followed and felt them with my entire being.

At 8 a.m., instead of cheerfully walking to school to meet my friends and learn new things, we were rushing to the basement of my mum's work (Mum works as a kindergarten teacher).

We spent the next thirteen days living in that basement.

For the first three days, there were seventy people living there with us: adults, children and old people. There were some vulnerable people who couldn't stand up on their own. There were also three dogs and a cat named Businka. Every time there was heavy shelling or loud explosions, the animals would hide under a pile of blankets.

We would wake up early and leave the kindergarten to go home because we needed to wash and cook some food. We also just really wanted to be at home. I spent every second missing it.

But after a while, we stopped being able to return home. It was too dangerous to leave the basement. The lights went out, it got really cold and there were fewer of us there, as those who were able to had left.

The first time it got really scary was when a missile hit a nearby block of flats, and the windows got blown out by the blast. Before then, the explosions were somewhere far away. Now, every day, another flat would burn down and every day, there were fewer and fewer of us in the basement. Many left because their homes had been destroyed, others simply left because it was getting too cold in the basement and the young children were beginning to fall ill.

In the morning, Mum, Dad and Grandad would go to the shop to try and fetch what food they could find. We would sprinkle some sugar on a piece of bread and pretend we were having a slice of Kyiv cake[48] with our tea.

We slept fully dressed on mattresses normally used by the kindergarten at nap time, but it was still very, very cold. Leaving the basement to get some fresh air was terrifying, especially if the shelling started while you were out there. You'd have to drop down to the ground. The shrapnel left marks on the school walls.

On day thirteen, the kindergarten was hit by a missile.

At that time, there were nineteen of us left in the basement – twelve adults, five children and two very old men aged eighty-nine and ninety-three, who were not able to walk. Most people were too scared to come here because the area was under constant shelling, but Dad found some volunteers who agreed to help us get out. We drove off towards the city centre, but it started getting bombed there too and, eventually, forty-three days after the war began, me, Mum and my brother fled to Western Ukraine.

Some of my favourite people – Dad, Granny and Grandad stayed behind in Kharkiv. I miss them terribly and I love them very much.

My greatest wish is for there to be peace!

Olha's Story

It had been an ordinary day. I was back home from school, doing my homework, chatting with my friends, playing with my cat. Towards the evening, I started to develop an earache. Mum and I decided that if the pain wasn't gone by morning, I wouldn't have to go to school. But my earache had nothing to do with why I didn't go to school the next day.

At 5 a.m., I was woken by a terrible explosion which I mistook for an earthquake at first. I was terrified and saw the look of horror on my parents' faces. I asked them about the explosions, and they said war had begun … I was in complete shock. My cat Busya was sitting next to me, as if offering comfort, even though the explosions must have scared her too. We started filling up bags and water bottles. In a panic, I began scooping everything off the table into a bag, but I knew that there was no way we could take all of it.

The explosions were getting louder and we were very frightened by the time we got down to the ground floor of our building. Down there, the explosions didn't seem so loud and it felt safer. Playing games on my phone made me feel like I was hiding behind a shield. I tried not to listen to the explosions, but they were deafening. However, despite the fear we felt, we kept trying to cheer each other up.

The phone calls and texts I was getting from my friends and family were also a good distraction. We stayed in the ground floor lobby of our building but, when things quietened down, we would pop back home to grab a bite to eat or to fetch something we needed. The next day, we went to the shop and had to queue for three hours. We filled an entire basket with food, but they started shelling again. The lights cut out and we all ran down to the shop's shelter. Once it was quiet, we rushed back home. That shop hasn't opened since.

With each passing day, it was getting more and more terrifying. We weren't running back up to our flat as often, because it was too frightening. We spent six days under constant shelling and explosions. It got especially terrifying when we heard aeroplanes flying in the sky and making turns right above us. That really frightened us. We couldn't bear spending another night in the ground floor lobby, so we had to sleep down in the hallway. In the morning, we gathered our things, including my beloved cat, and left the city.

The next day, our block of flats had a bomb dropped on it. We still dream of going home one day.

Kostya's Story

24 February: I shall remember that day forever! That was my last day at home! That was the day the war started.

I was woken up by explosions. One, two … a third … My parents woke up and couldn't understand what was happening. Only after looking out the window and seeing both the sky and the buildings by the ring road on fire did we realise that the worst had happened: war!

My little sister Tania was crying and Mum was trying to calm her down. I was very scared! We were paralysed with fear! Once we were dressed, my parents tried to decide what to do next. Where to go? I just wanted to get as far away from the explosions as possible!

We drove down to the centre of Kharkiv. My aunt works at a school there. A beautiful big old building designed way back when by Beketov[49] himself. There were loads of people gathered in the basement. Everyone was anxious and confused, no one knew what to do and what would happen next. The grown-ups turned the school gym into a sort of room for me and the other children. Mats were thrown on the floor for us to sit and sleep on, and even though the mums washed the floor it was still very dirty and very dusty.

Later that evening, we were joined by people from the neighbouring buildings. But they weren't alone, they had their pets with them. Now we had with us dogs, cats and even a hamster. Practically a whole zoo!

Some people slept on benches and chairs in the basement with the animals, while we slept in the school gym – we felt pretty safe there.

We could hear the explosions, some loud enough to pierce our hearts. We began to be able to tell if an explosion was close enough for us to need to brace, or if it was somewhere far away. On day six, we heard the sound of aeroplanes, and we got really scared. The horror around us was growing worse and worse.

We felt like our situation was hopeless.

We would always be accompanied by one of the parents when we left our 'kiddie bunker' to go to the bathroom or canteen.

The parents did their best to cheer us up: they'd come up with different games and activities. For example, I learned origami. However, despite the adults' best efforts, some of the children would still cry – scared by yet another *boom!* We would all try to help get them to settle down. We all lived as if we were one big family, even though some of us had never met before the war. We became each other's support system.

I spent eleven days in the school basement before driving out of the city with my parents, granny and my cat, Gilbert. I was shocked and upset seeing all the buildings that had been destroyed from our car window. You don't see that sitting in a basement! I was very surprised by the huge number of cars leaving the city. We spotted our friends in one of them, and we even had a few minutes to catch up. The mums cried!

Right now, I am in Central Ukraine where it's more or less safe. But every day the air raid alarms make us jump. Some say you can get used to anything. No! You can't get used to this!

I want to return home to Kharkiv! To see my friends and play outside, without having to hide from constant sirens and explosions! To go back to school, to see my teachers!

But, most of all, I want to see genuine smiles on my parents' faces again.

Alena's Story

On the morning of 24 February, I was awakened by a loud noise, which sounded like an explosion. I jumped out of bed and ran into my parents' bedroom and saw that they were up too. All I was told was, 'It'll all be all right, sweetie!'

I watched as Mum threw things into suitcases while Dad rushed out of the flat to go to the nearest petrol station.

The phone rang. It was my brother, asking where we were going. We decided to go to my grandmother's house. Before we left the flat, I managed to grab the teddy bear – our family mascot. Once outside, all I could hear and see were the screams and tears of the people standing on the street.

Then, I looked at my family and immediately felt better.

As there were a lot of us, we had to use two cars. The streets were packed; it was impossible to drive. But Dad knew a shortcut. I felt scared that I'd never come back home or see my friends again.

Finally, we arrived at Granny's house! It felt like it took an eternity to get here, even though it was only a ten-minute drive. The men went to get the basement in order and Mum, together with my aunt, drove to the shop to get food. It felt like things had settled down, but then I heard the phone ring and it was for my uncle, who worked as a border guard. He was going to war! My aunt was wailing and my brother, who had just recently completed his military service,[50] took my uncle aside and told him he'd be going with him. My uncle replied that he should stay and protect the family instead, and then began saying his goodbyes. I looked at my brother, who had tears streaming down his face. This strong, thick-skinned person was crying like a small child! I was crying too, but then my uncle came up to me, gave me a big hug and promised he would come back. He closed the door behind him and the room felt very empty all of a sudden.

Later, we heard another series of explosions. Everyone was grabbing their things and rushing to the basement. At first, we just stayed quiet and listened to the missiles flying over our house.

I was hugging my teddy, praying silently, believing that God would help us. My brother and my dad would go back out again from time to time to check the news. My aunt kept trying to reach my uncle, but he wouldn't pick up. We spent the rest of the day sitting in the basement, until the explosions finally died down. Then we went back to the house to have something to eat and went to bed.

In the morning, I woke up thinking that it was all just a bad dream, but I snapped out of it as soon as I heard my brother yelling that there were explosions again. And that's the way it was for a few days, up until the most horrifying day of my life.

The morning began as it usually would. We had breakfast and, at about 9 a.m., we heard the explosions again, so we rushed to the basement.

So here we are again, my whole family and my beloved

teddy, hiding in the basement. I saw my father and brother go outside and I hoped that meant we could go back to the house, where I could get back to reading my favourite Harry Potter book. But then I heard gunshots and a man's voice. They were ordering someone to surrender and said they only had one minute to do so. My brother and father ran back and told everyone to open their mouths[51] and put their heads down. Immediately after, we heard explosions. That was the sound of my father's school, which he attended as a child, being blown up. The school survived World War II but didn't survive 26 February 2022.

After a while, the explosions had died down and my brother and father left the basement, telling everyone to stay put. There was a strong smell of smoke in the air. When I was finally allowed to go outside, I thought I had arrived in hell: everything around us looked like it had been painted red and was covered in ash. That was the school burning. That's what the most horrifying day of my life was like.

Each day was no different from the last: always bad news and explosions. But I never lost heart, because I had my teddy with me.

One day, my dad and my brother decided that we were going to leave Kharkiv but they couldn't decide where to go. But then I heard the phone ring again – it was my uncle. He was safe and sound! After my dad and brother spoke to him, they said we should collect our things and that we were expected somewhere. It was late by now, 4 p.m., and the curfew was coming up, but my brother insisted we should get in the car and drive.

We left Granny's, but that wasn't the end of our problems. The explosions had blown the windshield off my brother's car, and there was rain and snow pouring in as we were driving. We were afraid we wouldn't make it!

I think my prayers helped us. We arrived at my uncle's friend's place in a village outside the city. There were over twenty people packed into that tiny house. They invited us to have some borsch[52] and pirozhki.[53] The night went by quietly and, for the first time in many days, I had a full night's sleep.

Next morning, we travelled until we reached Dnipro. There, we were met by some friends of my dad. They fed us and found us a place to live. Now we live next door to them.

I really want to go home, to see my friends and, most of all, I just want to hug my uncle! I am a child from Ukraine, my name is Alena, I am twelve years old and all I want is to have peace and be back at home!

My final note

When I read my friends' stories, I began to understand everything that they had been through ... everything they are still going through. The war has affected us all in so many different ways and hearing their descriptions of how their lives have suddenly changed made me realise that no two experiences are ever the same in situations like these. Seeing homes being burnt to the ground every day, wanting to go out for some air and suddenly getting caught in the shelling, being forced to sleep in cold, makeshift, unfamiliar surroundings like basements and schools – these are just some of the new and frightening events we've had to live through.

We couldn't believe that a war had really begun – it was all so alien: the noise of the explosions, the terror of shelling all around, the bombs being dropped on homes and schools.

The chaos is paining me to think of. The tears, the sorrow, the panic, the fear. There must be nothing more painful than watching a loved one go to war, not knowing whether they'll ever return.

We were all so thankful to have familiar faces around us – whether it was our family or pets. Small things like a slice of bread sprinkled with sugar or a comforting snuggle with a cuddly toy gave us something to cling on to. But the war was never far away.

I miss my friends very much, but I hope that we will all be able to meet up again one day and I truly wish that all of their hopes and dreams come true.

I want to finish by saying this: we are only children, and we deserve to live a life of peace and happiness!

Notes

General note on Yeva's diary:

Yeva speaks Russian and Ukrainian as is usual for Ukrainians who live near the Russian border. She writes mostly in Russian. Sometimes Yeva's diary entries are broken up into times that refer to when events happened earlier that day, and at other times the timing refers to when she wrote the entry. All events are as Yeva remembered them.

1. Kharkiv, or Khakov, where Yeva is from, is the second-largest city in Ukraine. It is in the north-east of the country and had a population of nearly 1.5 million people in 2021. It's a major cultural and industrial centre of Ukraine.

2. Freedom Square is the biggest city square in Ukraine and has held many major events such as concerts and fairs. The Derzhprom constructivist building stands at one end of the square. Built during Soviet times in 1928, it was known as the first Soviet skyscraper.

3. Military terminology has crept into the Ukrainian language and children sometimes use this in their play. This probably originates from the days of the Soviet Union when advances in military technology were seen as something to celebrate.

Day 2

4. Sumy is a city in north-eastern Ukraine, near the border with Russia. The battle of Sumy started on 24 February 2022 and involved the armies fighting on the streets until eventually Russia withdrew their troops from the area.

5. An armoured personnel carrier, also known as a 'battle taxi' because it transports infantry.

6. Eugenia Gapchinska is a Ukrainian artist who works in a whimsical style and calls herself the 'number one provider of happiness'. She is reported as being the highest paid artist in the country.

7. Pisochyn is a western district of Kharkiv.

8. Saltivka is a largely residential area in north-eastern Kharkiv.

9. A Grad system is a multiple launch rocket system designed to drop many missiles simultaneously. It is widely used by the Russian military and entered Soviet military service in the 1960s.

Day 3

10. Zmiiv is a city just south of Kharkiv.

11. Oleksii Potapenko is a Ukrainian singer and judge mentor on The Voice of Ukraine.

12. Schastia, Luhansk Oblast is a city in the east of Ukraine.

13. Oblast is the word for 'region' in Ukraine and the former Soviet Union.

14. Dnipro, previously called Dnipropetrovsk, is Ukraine's fourth largest city, located in central-eastern Ukraine on the Dnieper River after which it is named.

15. A traditional, sweet Slavic dish with a creamy, cheesy flavour and texture.

16. There have been widespread reports of Russian saboteurs hiding weapons in toys, mobile phones and other objects throughout Ukraine.

Day 4

17. A marker is a coloured light, dropped in an air-raid as a target indicator.

Day 5

18. 'As calm as a boa' is a common Russian saying meaning to keep calm under pressure.

Day 6

19. Okhtyrka is a 'Hero City' in the Sumy region of Ukraine. It is called a Hero City, a title awarded to ten cities in March 2022 for outstanding heroism during the invasion. There are four other Hero Cites in Ukraine already, which were named by the Soviet Union.

20. Also known as a thermobaric bomb, a vacuum bomb sets off two highly destructive explosions. The massive second blast is capable of vaporising human bodies.

21. Poltava is a small city located in the centre of Ukraine on the Vorskla River.

22. A submunition is a small weapon that is one of multiple submunitions contained in a larger weapon such as a cluster bomb or warhead.

23. A cluster bomb is a weapon containing multiple explosives dropped from aircraft or fired from the ground or sea, opening up in mid-air to release tens or hundreds of submunitions, which can saturate an area up to the size of several football fields. Anybody within the strike area of the cluster munition, be they military or civilian, is very likely to be killed or seriously injured.

24. The Geneva Conventions are four treaties, and three additional protocols, that establish international legal standards for humanitarian treatment in war. The singular term, 'Geneva Convention', usually denotes the agreements of 1949, negotiated in the aftermath of the World War II, which updated the terms of the two 1929 treaties and added two new conventions.

Day 7

25. Iryna and Yeva had a car but they weren't able to drive it out of Kharkiv because it was in a garage about a mile away from their flat and in need of a new battery.

26. Lviv is the largest city in Western Ukraine and one of the country's main cultural centres.

27. Red Cross volunteers in Ukraine provide support in a number of ways including supplying medicine and equipment, manning health centres and assisting people wanting to leave the country.

28. Checkpoints sprang up on roads throughout Ukraine after Russia invaded. Some of these are manned by the military, but lots are manned by volunteer residents of local towns and villages.

Day 8

29. Donetsk is an industrial city in eastern Ukraine, located on the Kalmius river in the disputed Donbas region.

Day 9

30. Zaporizhzhia is an industrial city in south-eastern Ukraine that is home to multiple power stations.

31. The Zaporizhzhia nuclear power plant is the largest in Europe and among the ten largest in the world.

32. Although Ukraine is geographically part of Europe, many countries that were part of the former Soviet Union don't consider themselves 'European', as there are still big cultural differences.

Day 12

33. Sovyne Hnizdo (Owl's Nest), is a historic wine cellar in Uzhhorod, often used as an event space. At the time Yeva was there, it was being used as a centre for refugee support.

34. Hryvnia or hryvnya has been the national currency of Ukraine since 1996. The hryvnia is subdivided into 100 kopiyky. The plural of hryvnia is hyrvni.

Day 13

35. Chop is a city in Western Ukraine, separated from the Hungarian town of Záhony by the river Tisza.

36. Although this is the version that was told to Yeva, Budapest actually got its name from two cities on opposite sides of the river Danube – Buda and Pest – merging. In Hungarian, 'Buda' means 'water' and 'Pest' means 'furnace'.

Day 15

37. Odessa is a seaport city in south-east Ukraine along the Red Sea.

Day 16

38. This is a small ritual that some people from former-Soviet countries do before going on a journey. As they're about to leave, they stop what they're doing and sit down – after a few seconds of sitting quietly they then leave. It is believed to have its origins in pagan times.

Day 18

39. Pupper is an affectionate term for a dog.

Day 20

40. The Book of Kells is an illuminated manuscript containing the four Gospels of the New Testament housed in Trinity College Library, Dublin.

Day 21

41. Chemical weapons are specialised munitions that use chemicals formulated to inflict death or harm on humans. Chemical weapons are classified as weapons of mass destruction.

Day 34

42. Sochi is a seaside town in Russia situated along the Black Sea.

Day 37

43. *The Steadfast Tin Soldier* is a fairytale written by Hans Christian Andersen in 1838 about a toy tin soldier who is stoic in the face of adversity.

Day 61

44. The Orthodox Easter celebrations in Ukraine would typically consist of family gatherings and festive dinners.

45. The USSR was an atheist state and so New Year replaced Christmas as the main winter celebration. Although Christmas is celebrated now (by Orthodox and Catholics), gifts are still exchanged at New Year.

Day 67

46. A second home used for summer holidays and common in former Soviet countries.

47. Penny buns are a mushroom with a large brown cap and bay boletes are an edible, pored mushroom found in woods in Europe and North America. Chanterelles are one of the most popular wild, edible mushrooms. They are orange, yellow or white and are funnel-shaped.

My Friends' Stories

48. Kyiv cake is a dessert consisting of sponge and meringue layers with hazelnuts, chocolate glaze and a buttercream-like filling.

49. Aleksey Nikolayevich Beketov was a Russian Imperial and Soviet architect. He was born in 1862 and died in 1941.

50. Military service for 12–18 months is compulsory for Ukrainian men aged eighteen.

51. The shockwave from an explosion creates a pressure wave in the body. If your mouth is closed the air in your ears and mouth cannot move freely and could rupture your eardrums. In extreme cases, the air in your lungs could rupture your lungs. Opening your mouth attempts to give this air a way to leave the body and minimize damage.

52. Borsch, also spelled borscht, is a sour soup typically made with beetroot, which gives it its distinctive red colour. It is a traditional dish in Ukraine, Russia and Poland, usually cited as originating in Ukraine.

53. Pirozhok (singular) or pirozhki (plural) are baked or fried yeast-leavened boat-shaped buns with a variety of fillings. They can be either savoury or sweet and are a popular street and comfort food.

Me and my Granny Iryna.
We're always together.

Acknowledgments

February 24. The day that changed my whole life.

The day that I began writing this diary. Whenever I felt paralysed by pain and fear, I would sit down and write. On these pages, I would share my feelings and it helped me cope. My goal was to put my experiences down in writing so that, ten or twenty years from now, I would be able to look back and remember how my childhood was destroyed by war.

I've met so many kind people during this difficult time, and I would like to dedicate these last few pages of my diary to them.

My beloved Granny Iryna has always stood beside me. She supported and protected me since the very first minutes of the war. Even when my hands were shaking with fear, I knew for certain that as long as I was with Granny, she would do everything in her power to keep me safe. I haven't been alive for all that long, but I've always trusted her. I'm so thankful for her.

It very quickly became clear that we weren't safe in our home neighbourhood and that we had to flee. Granny reached out to all her friends, but no one was able to help us. Except Inna. She agreed to take us in and to let us stay with her, in a part of Kharkiv where it was safer. I'm very grateful to her for taking care of me and for coming up with ways to distract me, like painting.

When we couldn't find a way to flee Kharkiv, and it seemed that all hope was lost, God sent us Todor and Oleh, two amazing volunteers who fearlessly agreed to take us to Dnipro. I thank them for their bravery and the kindness in their hearts. All through our journey, I met a lot of incredible people – Rada, Arsenyi, Myna, Father Emilio and Attila. These are all people with big, generous hearts.

The reporters from *Channel 4 News* – Paraic, Freddie, Flavian, Tom, Delara and Nik – have completely changed my life. When they heard my story and learned of this diary, they decided to help us in any way they could. They worked hard and, thanks to them, we were able to make it all the way to Dublin. These amazing, kind, brilliant and generous people are always prepared to help those in need. They have left a bright and warm little light deep within my soul.

In Dublin, we were welcomed by Catherine Flanagan and her family. After a long and difficult journey, my life had turned into a fairy tale. A beautiful house and a warm, cosy atmosphere. Gary has shown us around all the beautiful parts of Dublin. Catherine helped me enrol at the school she works at. They helped us during a very difficult time in our lives, and I am thankful to them.

I feel safe and at ease at my new school – as if I've always been a student here. I'm free to play the grand piano or go to one of the tennis courts and play tennis. The girls in my class gave me a very warm welcome and I've made lots of new friends. I'm grateful for their kindness and sincerity.

I would also like to express my gratitude to the owners of the house we're now living in. It's a beautiful home and we're very happy here.

I'm so thankful to God for meeting an amazing, beautiful woman – Marianne Gunn O'Connor, my agent. I could fill an entire chapter of this diary with how wonderful she is, but I'm especially grateful for her warmth, kindness, compassion and desire to help. The world needs more people like her. Having her as my agent is a great honour.

Thanks so much to Michael Morpurgo for his great support. It is a huge honour that he has paid attention to my book – and to my life. I will carry it with me always.

I am especially grateful to Bloomsbury for offering to publish this diary. The team there, especially Sally Beets, Lara Hancock, Katie Knutton, Beatrice Cross and Alesha Bonser, have all gone to great lengths to help me make a better life. The hard work they are doing to publish my book will give me a chance at education and happiness. With their help, I'm confident that things will work out for me. I'm so happy to be published by them.

I'm thankful to God as well as to the kind people I've met along the way. Everything will be all right. I believe in that!

If you'd like to help more people like Yeva and Iryna,
Bloomsbury Publishing invites readers to support the
work of UNHCR, the UN Refugee Agency.

Every donation, no matter how big or small, can help
make a difference for people fleeing conflict and persecution
around the world. Bloomsbury Publishing will match
donations raised up to £10,000.